TALES FROM MY
STETHOSCOPE

TALES FROM MY
STETHOSCOPE

True stories of life on the streets from a
not-too-serious paramedic

BRUNA DESSENA

Quickfox
publishing

Published by Quickfox Publishing
PO Box 50660 West Beach 7449
Cape Town, South Africa
www.quickfox.co.za
info@quickfox.co.za

First edition 2010
Second edition 2017

TALES FROM MY STETHOSCOPE
ISBN 978-0-620-46851-0 (Second edition)

www.tales-from-my-stethoscope.com
www.publisher.co.za

Overwriter – Daphne Stokoe
Editor – Rachel Bey-Miller
Cover and book designer – Vanessa Wilson
Typesetting and production – Quickfox Publishing
Printing – Quickfox Publishing, Cape Town

**NOTE: As this book is based on true stories, identifying details
have been changed to protect the anonymity of those involved.**

"If I have seen further, it is by standing on the shoulders of giants."

– Sir Isaac Newton

DEDICATION

I would not be where I am today if it were not for the giants in my life who gave me love, encouragement and spurred me on, no matter how big or small my dream was.

To my beautiful children, Themba and Khangi – a little something to remember your Mamma Bruna by.

To my Brother Marco and Sister Lisa who love me unconditionally, and who offer their unwavering support with open arms.

To Daphne, my overwriter and initial editor, who gently reminded me about a wonderful function called "spell-check" and who never minded when I did not use it.

To Rachel Bey-Miller who took the final manuscript, organised the content and made it palatable (without my many expletives and sarcasm) and produced a work I am proud to say is mine.

To my partner and publisher, Vanessa, for all her hard work on both my books. She does not realise the importance of her work – making peoples' dreams come true – which she does with such good humour, attention and dedication. Thank you.

To my students, especially Darren van Zyl, who have surpassed the master and continue to teach me so much, with such integrity.

To the doctors who took the time to teach me with patience and generosity.

To every dedicated person in emergency medicine who have chosen the most noble of careers and who, above all else, practise the profession honourably – they leave an indelible mark in the lives of the patients they treat.

Contents

1

The Saturday Night Show

BEFORE an artist can paint a picture, he needs a canvas on which to paint. And then he needs a palette of colours; mixing a little of this and some of that to give us something entirely different, something we've never seen before. And it's the same with stories. Before I can tell you the individual little cameos, I need to give you the large, background canvas on which the smaller details will leave their imprint.

And so, for starters, I proudly present – complete with glitz and glamour – the Saturday Night Show, brought to you by the colourful citizens of Johannesburg! Every week I have watched them walking, stumbling and being dragged into casualty. This is the longest-running real, live show in the city. There are always more than enough players for the lead and supporting roles, and plenty of aspiring stars waiting in the wings.

The roles are many and varied and most original; just when I think I've seen it all, another little cherub does something spectacular. Like the security guard who came into casualty with a deep, horizontal gash across his forehead, caused by his forgetting a minor detail – that his hand was still cuffed to the money box when he threw it into the back of the van with all the enthusiasm of an Olympic shot-put athlete.

The Comedy Award invariably goes to one of a number of characters who are fuelled by booze, stupidity, or both – those who think: "It will never happen to me; I won't get caught." This includes the semi-bald men with their compensatory ponytails, who cannot hold their drink, but drip titanium jewellery and generally suffer from a serious case of arrested adolescence as they perch on oversized Harleys, surveying the world beyond their protuberant stomachs. And so too the young men armed with raging hormones and elephant-sized egos, strutting their stuff around swimming pools, their trademark the inevitable badly cut jeans. They always arrive in massive 4x4s, ramping pavements.

Surprisingly, other members of the 'stupid, booze-fuelled team' include well-dressed women driving expensive cars, flaunting Jenna Clifford jewellery, their brains soaked in Chivas Regal. And, of course, students on the last day of exams, letting rip, burning their books, and their boats.

Not to be outdone, there are also the Friday Night Actors (the ones who get paid weekly), who never let us down. When you have worked as a paramedic as long as I have, you know the routine. Friday nights start out relatively quietly. By 11 pm when the weekly pay has all gone to the *shebeen*[1] around the corner, the fun starts. Radios in response cars, ambulances and police vehicles scream into life in and around Johannesburg, and all the major cities of our rainbow nation.

---

1   An unlicensed drinking establishment

"Juliet 28, make your way to Jeppe and Loveday for a pedestrian. Romeo 01, I have an assault for you in Bertrams," and the daily expectation, "Make your way to Hillbrow for a shooting."

Like clockwork the crews eat early, grabbing a bite at the local garage where the best Wild Bean coffee is served; then we await the Friday Night Show, precursor to the Saturday Night Show. Let's take a look at the nominees, shall we? The Stupidity Awards are hotly contested between those who think they can drive while under the influence, sometimes with an accessory, such as a gun or an equally drunk wife, and those who think they are on the set of a James Bond movie.

Following closely on their heels are those who are victims of, or participants in, our very popular sport – Senseless Violence. Violence in our country is led by the champion team in Hillbrow, but not far behind are the southern-suburbs with their quasi-trailer-trash Weekend Warriors. No one beats them for originality, and the use of new weapons and staying power when it comes to killing or dying. They have the big boys on their team – the Nigerian drug lords, Lebanese gangs and even bigger gangs indigenous to that region, like the Portuguese boys and their protégés.

Violence is part of our everyday lives. It is constantly being thrust on us in various forms – in art, advertising, bestsellers and on television. It's unconsciously promoted, even in innocuous channels like news, satellite, reality shows and good old family entertainment, in varying degrees. We see endless music videos, courtesy of MTV, teaching children that men in oversized prison gear are something to aspire to.

It always has great entertainment value to brag to your mates how the cops chased you down Louis Botha Avenue in peak-hour traffic, or how you managed to keep an ambulance behind you and wouldn't let it pass.

Make-up comprises various shades of dried blood, vomit, black-and-blue bruising and swollen lips courtesy of a choice of options –

drunk and disgruntled husband; connecting with a windshield; jealous boyfriend or girlfriend; and last, but not least, hijackers and muggers.

Best Actor's Award goes to the men pretending to be sober, the men caught with their pants down and trying to convince their not-so-smiley spouse, "It's not what it looks like" or "I can explain."

A Special Award must go to the innovative moron who at 3 am fell through the roof of a warehouse and told us he was looking for a job. Award for Best Actress goes to one of those women (Chivas Regal-soaked brains) who try sweet-talking the traffic police that they "really only had one, officer."

Up-and-coming stars are gangsters from Westbury, Fitasdorp and Turffontein who talk tough, with close contenders the tow-truck guys. There is stiff competition here for the widest swagger, closely followed by those strange all-male bonding rituals known as arm-wrestling, snapping beer bottle caps with teeth and the eternal foul-mouthing that includes insulting mothers in some form – the favourite being "Your mother swam out to a warship…"

The porters at the hospitals get the award for Creepiness. There's just something about them. Best Costumes go to the security forces – guys who are kitted out as if for Armageddon; and women in curlers with ill-fitting vests and skirts so short one stares in fascination.

Special Effects goes to flying vehicles that wrap themselves around poles; blocks of flats that are partially destroyed by a gas oven having been left on; a man flattened under a car because he did a terrible job of setting the car on paint buckets to work on the exhaust; cars that land in swimming pools; babies and children mauled by vicious dogs; and people with hands caught in the mincer in a hotel kitchen.

Awards in the Horror department go to those who let their children plummet thirteen floors onto a picket fence; those who don't wear seatbelts; those who were asleep when the house caught alight …

And let's not forget the numerous contenders for the ever popular Gunshot Head. Ah yes, South Africa leads in this category, thanks to the number of guns we have floating around in the wrong hands.

Honours go to the brave South African Police Flying Squad members, the dog units that endanger their lives every day and the helicopter pilots with nerves of steel, who chase hijackers from on high.

These awards would not be given out without those great contributors who make it all possible, players in a multi-million Rand industry – alcohol manufacturers and distributors. Those wonderful enterprises that supply tons of the liquid responsible for oiling the darker side of the human machine, for turning ordinary men and women into violent, blubbering, sometimes really puerile offenders, and university students into rude and vomiting heaps of miscreants. Sophisticated people go from hero to zero in less than two hours; these substances change hard, competent men and women who can normally run huge businesses into two-year-olds throwing expensive tantrums. Ask any paramedic: "In terms of disgusting behaviour, who are the worst offenders?" I am willing to bet money on it, it'll be drunk patients every time.

* * *

One happy Sunday morning, and one of the first weekend shifts I was on duty, a call came in as a 'domestic in progress'. Now this can mean many things, depending largely on location. If it's in the northern suburbs, it means wife has found out about husband's indiscretion and is hurling the Swarovski crystal and phoning her personal coach and lawyer faster than you can say botox. He, meanwhile, is holding his head in shame, ill-fitting toupee askew.

If the call comes from the south, things get noisy and colourful. Here there is no holding back, or as the saying goes, "we take no prisoners." One almost feels sympathy for the errant spouse who loses everything, including what little dignity he has left after the entire block of flats has heard about his indiscretion, lurid details of the sexual favours she's done him and how she's received nothing but a drunk low-life bum in return.

On arrival, the first things one sees are all his clothes, tools, playing cards, condoms and horseracing books strewn on the lawn, much to the entertainment of the neighbours. Think of these as props for the show about to unfold. Sometimes there is also a couch, but couches are sacred and, being sacred, they rarely become a casualty of this war. The couches are generally dark brown or dark green. Very seldom do they have patterns on them, and they are never leather. There are a lot of these couches in neighbourhoods of this kind and I've never quite figured out why they are endemic to the south.

Now the old-faithfuls rock up. The Bystanders never let you down – they are there shouting encouragement to her. In some areas the neighbours get very involved and they start to throw objects – whatever comes to hand. By this stage the men have started to identify with the husband and take sides, and the war moves into Phase Two where the protagonists are the toothless men against the women in curlers and ill-fitting vests, covering large, braless breasts.

What is particularly interesting is there is no order to the sides, no fence, no uniforms – so there are little skirmishes on both sides of the house. By now no one remembers which domestic scene was the original, who the combatants were, or where exactly ground zero of this war is. Many times it moves into Phase Three where the police arrive and try to negotiate but that is as effective as trying to stop a wave rolling in on the shore. Phase Four is my favourite, when the focus moves drastically – the victim and perpetrator unite and start to assault the police, and reinforcements are hastily called for, by both sides.

The kids are in the background observing closely and taking notes for the time when they will be called upon to do this traditional dance.

Phase Five is the anticlimax when the motley crew get transported to the police station in the same van and, if they are unlucky enough, get to spend the night in the cells where much making up takes place. Then they're all ready to do it again next payday. Don't you just love the Saturday Night Show?

* * *

Most paramedics love their calling. We are on top of the world when we receive a 'good call'. We get that noticeable spring in our steel-toe-capped boots.

So what defines a good call? A good call requires the paramedic to feel that adrenalin rush as you get dispatched, figuring out the shortest route to your destination. You fly like a bat out of hell, dodge taxis and slow vehicles, run the gauntlet in peak-hour traffic, arrive at the call, assess the situation, make a quick decision, haul out every piece of equipment that squeals, bleeps and flashes, then proceed to remember drug dosages, pray hard, deal with screaming passengers and upset family members, and while all this is going on, look cool and in control.

I suppose it's very much like the surfer always waiting for the perfect wave – that all-defining, death-defying, mind-boggling, life-altering wave. Just when you think that was it, there is a little voice that nags at the back of the cerebellum and taunts, "Yes, but what if there was a better one, a greater one, the one that defies all logic, all science or reason? The one that elevates you amongst your peers, leaving an indelible mark under ICON in their mental filing systems. If you stop now, you will never know."

In case there are readers finishing school soon who are uncertain about a choice of career, let me tell you what it entails.

If you think it might be 'a nice job' you must realize that it's a very tough one, needing complete dedication – and lots of guts. But to me, it's one of the most noble of professions. South Africa might be behind other countries in some areas, but we undoubtedly have the best paramedics in the world. This is because we are exposed to so much trauma that we have built up the confidence to treat serious trauma injuries without blinking an eye. One only has to see the number of foreign doctors who come here to do their elective (two years' internship in a State hospital) at major trauma hospitals like Baragwanath (now Chris Hani Hospital) in Soweto. In one 12-hour shift it's practically guaranteed that a medical student will see at least one stab wound, a gunshot wound, and plenty of HIV patients. And if it's the Saturday Night End-of-the-Month Show, the gunshots and assault-related traumas will escalate according to the drink consumed and the lateness of the hour.

The New Year's Eve Show

It was always a blast to work in Hillbrow on New Year's Eve. It really was a great way to make memories and get your adrenalin kick. Sadly, the fairly innocuous frolics of days gone by have been replaced by shootings and are not much fun. In the old days, the Berea fire station would be used as a makeshift triage[2] area as it was strategically well placed for both the Hillbrow Hospital and Johannesburg General Hospital (colloquially referred to as the Joburg Gen). We would send only the serious cases to these hospitals as they would already be inundated; we dealt with the less serious cases at the fire station. The medics would be falling over themselves to work on New Year's Eve – did I mention I love my job?

---

2   The process of sorting patients according to urgency of illness or injury

New Year's Eve meant Action with a capital A. For sure, some poor sod would be flung from some or other balcony. There would be at least five gunshot wounds, plus a few stabbings and a minimum of 20 motor vehicle accidents, all of which would be alcohol-induced. It's a sad time of year for people on their own, and there would certainly be a couple of people who'd decided that this is the year they end it all. Then, of course, the over-exertion and overeating would bring on one or two coronaries, just to make the mixture more interesting.

People are the same the year round. The same cast that entertains us on the Saturday Night Show, appear again in the New Year Event – only this time, it's the new, improved version. We will see people dive into swimming pools with the covers still on; others will slide down cars that have been converted into 'foofy' slides using soapy water, resulting in the odd guy here and there having his scrotum unexpectedly divided into four sacs – lucky chaps.

With so much energy needing expression, people will get up and dance on tables forgetting they're made of glass; and a real highlight of the evening could be when they discover the fun of lighting each other's farts close to an open bottle of highly flammable liquid. I remember one year a woman caught her orthodontic brace in her husband's pierced penis. If there isn't enough noise, someone might decide to pop off a few shots; it happened once that someone discharged all five rounds into the ceiling – only to find out his friend was in the room above him shagging the next-door neighbour. The bullets narrowly missed him and he lived to tell the tale – many, many days later.

I have seen people want to swim with the fishes because the marijuana said so, so they try to climb into the fish tank – why not?

Large batches of dagga cookies are baked in kitchens all over Hillbrow, enough to provide for a forthcoming famine. Everyone eats them, including the dog ... and unattended children who find them and end up flying higher than a Boeing.

Inside houses both dirt poor and modest, we get to see unbelievable things during New Year. There is the brainless guy who places super glue on the toilet seat for a laugh; the kinky couple who has sex on rubber sheets with oil all over their bodies and, yes folks, so well oiled is she that she slides right off the bed and smashes into the glass bedside table. A slippery little fish too difficult to hold – smelling of lavender oil. And let's not forget the macho man who flings his wife up into the rotating ceiling fan …

This is the New Year's Eve Show, which has even more innovative stunts than the Saturday Night Show. Every year at the same time, it never lets you down. And, as you'd expect, sponsored by the biggest breweries in South Africa.

Nowadays there are a few diehards who still choose the New Year shift, but it's not the same. The crowd is not the same. We don't go into Hillbrow anymore, it's too dangerous. We wait on the outside and a private security company goes in and brings the patients to us. No more congregating at Highpoint and kissing total strangers Happy New Year; now we just sit on the outskirts and listen to the gunshots and wait for the crackers at midnight, marking the passage of another year.

I remember past years in my response car, in front of Highpoint, wishing the jubilant crowd "Happy New Year" on the P.A. system. I recall the joy of being there, the wonderful feeling of sharing it with so many strangers who meant you no harm, the way they rocked the car and shouted "happy, happy". It's sad that those days are now long gone.

* * *

2

Becoming qualified

YOU might be wondering how one becomes a paramedic? In South Africa – until not too long ago – there were three levels of medics – BLS (Basic Life Support), ILS (Intermediate Life Support) and ALS (Advanced Life Support). The Health Professions Council of South Africa only allowed you to call yourself a paramedic if you held the ALS qualification.

There were two paths to qualifying. If you were fortunate enough to have the funds to pay for full-time tuition, the one option was to obtain a National Diploma or B.Tech degree. These courses consisted of a lot of theory, much of it in great depth, particularly in the degree course.

If you chose the other option, as I did, you joined the public service as a civil servant in the Emergency Services and did a combination of short courses with practical on-the-road experience. Within the first six months you'd have to pass your BAC (Basic Ambulance Attendants Course). This was a four-week course, during which the candidate learned how to deal with all medical and trauma cases on a basic level – meaning nothing invasive was done to the patient. Ambulance attendants were recognized by the qualification badge they wore on their uniform. If, having achieved the BAC, the student decided to go to the next level, they were required to complete 1 000 hours on the road, working in an ambulance, not in a hospital – and they had to be able to prove that they'd done those hours.

The next step was to write an entrance exam and, if accepted, attend the course on the next level – the ILS (Intermediate Life Support) course. This was a two-month course at the end of which the graduate was allowed to dispense five different drugs, and was competent enough to place an intravenous line on a patient.

If the student chose to go ahead and do the ALS (Advanced Life Support) course, they were required to have at least 2 000 hours working with the ambulance crew. It must be said that this job was not for sissies! The entrance exam was tough and the average pass rate was 61%. This might sound harsh, but in South Africa we didn't have enough doctors – certainly not enough to have them out on the road. The ALS paramedic was the backup for any crew needing assistance. We didn't need a doctor with us, as there was not much more any doctor could do pre-hospital, other than unique procedures that are often not done on the road, such as inserting a chest drain in a patient who is bleeding rapidly into his chest cavity, which requires a sterile environment. Sometimes doctors were sent with the helicopter crew when it was truly an emergency. Our doctors are generally excellent; in our country they need to be confident treating trauma patients. At Baragwanath Hospital, fourth-year medical students are opening up chests in less than four minutes, something only consultants[3] are allowed to do overseas.

---

3   The term 'consultant' applies to a specialist, for instance a cardio-thoracic surgeon.

Our ALS qualification was – and remains – on the same level as the Americans – those guys we see in the movies, coming to the rescue. We use the same drugs and equipment; in fact, our textbooks are American! One difference, though: with America being such a litigious society, the American ALS paramedic or EMT (Emergency Medical Technician) has to confirm their administration of drugs before giving them, for fear of being sued.

In South Africa, the system of qualifying has now changed. The short courses have fallen away and been replaced by the ECA (Emergency Care Assistant), a one-year national certificate course; the ECT (Emergency Care Technician), a two-year diploma course; and the ECP (Emergency Care Practitioner), a four-year Bachelor of Emergency Care degree. Should the ECP wish to further advance, they can complete various Masters and Doctorate programmes.

Doing away with the short courses in my opinion is ludicrous in a country where there are so many economically disadvantaged people who will not be able to afford to go to a Technikon. Previously, most of these people would have done the four-week Basic Ambulance Attendant's course (BAC) and been of tremendous help to their communities by filling a gap that is already straining under the pressure of limited human resources. The decision to phase out the short courses will therefore hurt the very people who need help most.

It must also be said that one of the major advantages of qualifying on the job by way of short-courses was that, by the time the National Diploma and B.Tech students had obtained their qualifications, the rest of us had already clocked up many thousands of hours of practical road experience and become proficient at dealing with both the medical and the human side of attending to calls. And nothing beats real on-the-job mentoring by those special souls who've been around the block a bit.

Our paramedics are confident, experienced and not afraid of huge scenes. We don't need twenty-minute coffee breaks because a union insists on it; we do the work because we love it – and there is always a chocolate bar to fill the gap when we don't get time to eat. Sadly, the majority of ALS paramedics work out of the country because, like all core structures in our country, we are very poorly paid. At the last count, of the 1 800 registered in the country, only 370 work on the road in South Africa.

The law on the certification of death has changed. ALS paramedics now have the authority to declare a patient dead at a scene, and sign a legal document to this effect. This has become not only feasible but necessary, as there are various tests we carry out to make certain that the patient is dead and not hypothermic. It has happened in the past that if the pupils in the eye didn't respond, the pulse was difficult to find and the person basically seemed lifeless, a policeman with no medical knowledge declared the person dead and the body would be taken away and dumped at the morgue. Sometimes the patient had merely fallen asleep on a cold concrete floor and hypothermia had set in. After a while, the body would become warm and the 'corpse' would come back to life, causing much embarrassment and loads of paperwork, not to mention sending the traumatized patient into arrhythmia. Patients are declared dead when they are warm and dead – that is the golden rule.

Looking back on my life, I don't regret a moment of it. Growing up, I had various ideas of what I wanted to do, as do all young people. And I, in fact, did do some other things. But the decision to be a paramedic is one that enables me to wake up every morning with a happy, fulfilled heart.

* * *

Student days

I finished school in 1982, worked four years as a dental assistant, followed by a couple of other things and entered the paramedic field in a class of ten young men – I was the only woman. I went into the Ambulance Division and worked my way up to being an ALS in 1994. I decided to do something different just for a short while, so I took a break for two years and qualified as an Oral Hygienist when I was 36. That was quite an experience, being in a class with girls who were not even born when I matriculated!

I loved my time at varsity; Wits is a great university. Every morning I would arrive early and sit at Senate House and have a cappuccino and read the paper. I was surrounded by places steeped in history. Beautiful old buildings, students whose parents had possibly been students there themselves in the days when things were really exciting; when people rioted for worthwhile causes. In the days of Trevor Huddleston, Miriam Makeba, Helen Joseph, Steve Biko and the likes. This was the university that trained principled men and women who shaped our great country; those who stood against enormous adversity and led the field in so many different ways in the sedulous and steady forging of their paths.

I wasn't sorry that I was the ripe old age of 36 when doing my Diploma. I could really appreciate the art galleries, the music concerts, and the huge library with the biggest painting I have ever seen called *Takama Adamastor*. I loved sitting on the great steps and watching the students go by, like one sometimes does when sitting at a quaint bistro, with no rush on one's time and ample opportunity to study the everyday habits and body language of the patrons and passers-by. And my best of all, the Wits film library where I could watch old movies during my off periods. And yes, I actually did do some studying and qualified in 2001.

When I was in my second year of studying Oral Hygiene, I had the privilege of working on the Pelopepa train. This was a train that was on the tracks for nine months of the year, stopping in different towns all over the country every week, dealing with various illnesses and specializing in mouth and eye problems. The community of each town would be told beforehand when the train was coming, and patients would start lining up long before sunrise.

When I had my week on the train, it stopped at the scenic town of Sabie in Mpumalanga. Amongst the medical personnel on board were a dentist, dental students, oral hygiene students, student community nurses, and optometry students.

If I'd previously thought my work was humbling, it couldn't compare with what I saw happening in the optometry department. To watch a myopic patient enter the first carriage, where she had her eyes tested, then sit in the second carriage, waiting while a student, under supervision, cut her glasses; and finally emerge out of the last carriage, bewildered but hopeful. And then – to be handed a Bible, and be able to read the small print! The tears of happiness on those faces were enough to reduce me to an emotional heap. To be part of that was a privilege indeed. It is a real shame that those student days are long gone.

* * *

When I was in my first year in the service, it was normal for the men to try to scare the women either with the grotesqueness of the situation or the patient's injuries. I remember they always made the newcomers sit in the back of an ambulance with a body bag or a dead patient on a stretcher.

The first time you visited the morgue they would lock you in the fridge with all the bodies. I remember so clearly looking up from my clipboard and being confronted by a sea of bodies all around me, naked and on open steel shelves; stacked, some on top of each other. Old, young, black, white, completely burned, limbs missing, old people and babies, thin, fat, the list goes on and on.

After the initial shock of realizing where I was, a strange calmness descended on me – a feeling of standing on hallowed ground. I felt ashamed of my colleagues' brazen callousness; these bodies were once dignified humans who would have covered up; this man would have tilted his hat at a lady, and that one would have bowed his head in greeting to his granny. Yet here they were literally thrown together, stripped of everything, every piece of clothing, every object humans use to hide behind, like the oversized Gucci sunglasses, the loud swearing, the bragaccio attitude, the 'do you know who I am' thinking, the hood worn within the 'hood, the tattoos that display who you owe allegiance to, the colours of your motorbike gang, the giving-the-finger sign, the highly decorated uniforms that once bristled with shiny guns, the skinheads snarling at conformity … here they were all equal, all together. I was the one outside, the one who didn't fit in … the one who, no matter what I did, would eventually have to give up and leave everything too. I too would look like this. I too would finally be without inhibition and really not care who gazed at me. I too would not have to worry about my love handles, my scars and imperfections that society made me believe really counted and were the ultimate yardstick to being a better, smarter, more sexy, more desirable me – the ultimate round peg fitting in a round hole.

* * *

When I was a student, we were required to complete a certain number of road shifts. This involved having one or two instructors in the response car with you and your 'practical partner.' You were dispatched on calls and were evaluated on your performance, command of the scene, knowledge of drugs and dosages, application of that knowledge, and so on. It was a very tense time, as you can imagine. I was completing my road pracs for my CCA (Critical Care Attendant – the ALS qualification) level when we were doing one of these shifts. We had arrived back at the building (where Daisy de Melker once nursed!) to restock and the next call was to be my partner, Stephen's, call.

We had both gone upstairs to fetch disposable equipment. He was then called back to the car, while I was left behind to clean equipment and restock. I remember collecting the various goods and switching off the lights. I then sat outside on the small wall and waited for the crew to come back from their call. After a while, I noticed the lights were on in the corridor where I had just been. Not thinking, I went back into the building, opened the heavy front door, walked down the corridor and called out.

It struck me then that nobody could have walked past me to open the door without my seeing or hearing them. I switched off the lights again and resumed my position on the low wall outside. Sure enough, in a while, they went on again.

I'm not easily scared, but I'm terrified of ghosts. I suppose it's the fact that I can't control or hold them that makes me afraid of them. I have been told by people who have encountered them that it's not as scary an experience as one would think. But knowing that this was where a famous poisoner had strolled the corridors made me do a quick rethink. When the crew returned, my instructor asked me to switch off the lights. I explained that I already had, twice, and how very odd it was that they had gone on again. Not a chance was I going back in there to switch them off again!

* * *

I will always have the fondest memories of the Brixton fire station where I began my career. Ah yes, I'm showing my age. In those long-ago days, we wore white coats over our uniforms. And unbelievably, in those days the calls came in on one land-line phone. The station officer would write details on a loose piece of paper, or tear off a piece of newspaper; then put his head out the office door, whistle or scream some invective, and add his favourite – Balletjies (little balls) or Meisie (little girl).

The ambulances were lined up in convoy outside, ready to go. The driver would come by, the medic would grab the slip and they would be on their way. Those were the days when there were many ambulances on shift and not enough ALS paramedics in the city – there were only five that we knew of.

Learning from others

I worked with some interesting characters back then. I remember E, who was not a small woman, and who thought nothing of leaping out of the ambulance while it was still going, to grab a bag snatcher. She would beat him to a pulp and then hand him over to her colleagues to fix.

Then there was N who had missed his calling in life. He should have been a priest; he would get to a call and have endless religious discussions with the patient while the poor soul was bleeding to death in front of him.

Most unforgettable was J. A fitness fanatic, this man would eat an onion in his ambulance like most people eat an apple. However, that wasn't the most astounding thing about him. His gift was that he was always calm, slow and very controlled; nothing stressed him. He refused to use a siren, preferring to only have lights on, and on the way to a call – wait for it! – he had a whistle in his mouth. He would go through intersections slowly with red lights on and a whistle in his mouth, using hand signals to stop traffic. When I sat next to him I constantly observed the puzzled expressions of the oncoming motorists. Then upon arrival at a call, he would haul out his trusty well-worn tape measure and measure the patient against the spine board, with the distressed family members looking on in shock. He would be wide awake all night doing crossword puzzles, and never seemed to nod off.

A was a good friend who was always ready with a trick up her sleeve and game for anything that involved a lot of laughter. One Sunday she walked into Cardies and bought one of those fake arms, which she then shut in the back of the ambulance door. She flew off to the next call with the offending arm waving at all the cars behind the ambulance, until some member of the public put a stop to it by phoning the station officer. Some people just have no sense of humour!

L was a fantastic paramedic, another one of those you felt very safe being around. She was scared of nothing, I tell you – not even a Parktown prawn. One afternoon there was a call – a snake bite. It was a helicopter call and she was on duty that day. After treating the patient and stabilizing him for his flight to Baragwanath Hospital, someone at the scene mentioned that the snake was still in the kitchen cupboard. Not missing a beat, L grabbed a pillowcase from the heli and cajoled the reptile into her trap. She then climbed into the heli and they flew to the hospital – with an extra occupant on board in the pillowcase.

On arrival they walked past hundreds of people, both patients and their supporting family members, all waiting to be treated. When they got to the bed to hand over the snake-bite victim, there were about seven people standing around, waiting to watch the procedure. This is a teaching hospital so there are always more than enough people to help and even more to stand by doing nothing. They reached the point when the senior doctor asked if they knew what type of snake was responsible for the bite. Right on cue, L nonchalantly hauled out the offending snake by its throat and said, "I believe this is a puff adder." Freeze frame. Everyone turned to stone before all hell literally broke loose. There was only one door out of resus and there were at least twenty hysterical doctors, beyond-hysterical *mafuta*[4] sisters and a few patients lying on some of the other beds who were unlucky enough to

---

4   Hefty; big-boned; large

be awake and witness the writhing snake. Well, you do the maths and use your visualizing skills.

Imagine a number of *mafuta* Sisters all trying to squeeze out of the door at the same time, dropping files and syringes and other vital paraphernalia as they did so; there were patients running with drip stands attached, and some who had ripped out their drips rather than be in a room with a puff adder. It was reported that a patient three bays away heard the commotion while being sutured above his eye; he came flying out with a long suture thread trailing behind him as he headed for the exit.

As the patients in the waiting area heard the sisters shouting that famous *"Yo yo imama weh"* they followed just as quickly out the door. There were visiting doctors from Germany and Holland, who, not understanding the language, but knowing they were practising medicine in a violent country, needed no encouragement to scram – adding to the serious hysterical bottleneck making for the front entrance. The area in casualty was cleared more quickly than you could say Nerve Gas.

For a long time after that small incident there was very little need for the medic to do crowd control when bringing in a case. When the heli landed, the word was out via the grapevine that the heli carried a woman who handled snakes like no one's business.

* * *

In the course of my career I have had the privilege of lecturing and working at the Ambulance Training College. I say 'privilege' with sincerity because it's not everyone who gets this chance.

Every now and then situations arise where one is surprised at how literally students sometimes take things. One such incident happened when I was teaching a CPR class. I was trying to convey to the students that the dolls were very life-like and that if you could manage to raise the chest in the CPR doll called Resus Annie, then in real life you would be successful in delivering the adequate volume of breaths needed to resuscitate a patient. I also explained that the dolls are so life-like that the sternum where you do chest compressions really is that hard and yet pliable.

One doll we used had differently dilated pupils in its eyes – one was a blown pupil to show a no-brain response while the other eye showed normal function. I showed the class the eye that was blown, not realizing that a particular student was paying extreme attention. When I had finished my minute of CPR, I reiterated that after one minute of good CPR, the eyes would respond like this example, and then proceeded to show the other eye. This particular student was convinced that the doll really was life-like, so much so that, when it came to exams, he presented himself very seriously in front of me and three other instructors. We waited patiently as the student gathered himself, walking around the doll a few times. Sensing that he was nervous I said, "When you are ready, treat this resus as just a medical patient, normal CPR, for a minute."

Again we watched him scrutinizing the doll and eventually my colleague G asked "What are you looking for?"

He answered, "The paper roll."

Let me explain. On some of the old CPR dolls there is a roll of paper that comes out of the side of the doll with a graph that shows if your compression rate and depth are correct.

I said, "It's okay, this particular doll does not have the paper."

It was clear that he was still very agitated, and couldn't start his procedure. I told him, quite testily by then, to just forget the paper and start the procedure as there were a number of students waiting to be examined.

It turned out later that he had done a few shifts on the road and during one of these shifts he had attended a resuscitation. He had done compressions on the patient and I had then arrived on the scene and, after doing all the checks and realizing that the patient had passed away, terminated the resus. I never realized that I should have explained that there was nothing more one could have done to help that particular patient. The student was very upset at the time – he was convinced that the paper roll would come out of the patient to tell him if his CPR had been performed correctly or not. Since there was no paper roll, he had no way of knowing this, leaving him wondering if he was responsible for the death. So now, here he was at the exam, too nervous to start, already feeling like a failure.

Looking back, I couldn't recall that there had been anyone at that resus who was upset. Had I noticed then that he was genuinely disturbed, I would have pointed out to him that one of the hardest lessons for a qualified medic to learn is that despite all our gallant efforts, despite all the training, all the years of experience, when that cross in the Book of Life is ticked off, there is nothing more you can do. That is the hardest lesson of all.

I might add that some people, despite all the passion in the world, are just not made for paramedical work and he was not. He was taken off the road and put to work in a different section in the emergency services.

Assessing a scene

When a paramedic arrives at a scene, there is a set procedure they follow. First they do a primary survey, which includes checking the patient's level of consciousness, opening and maintaining an airway, looking and listening for adequate breathing and correcting it, and checking the pulse. Then they do a secondary survey, checking vital signs, doing a head-to-toe survey of the patient, and taking the patient's history. This phase includes treatment of injuries such as burns, bleeding, fractures and so on. Thirdly, the paramedic 'packages' the patient to prepare him or her for transport. Some patients are conscious and can be transported sitting up; others are strapped to a spine board and tightly packaged for air evacuation, or so that they can be transported laterally in an ambulance, to protect their airway. The last step is handing the patient over to a doctor in casualty or whoever will be responsible for continuing the patient's treatment.

Sometimes the cameras on cellphones prove to be of inestimable value in recording the details of an accident. They are being used more and more by medics bringing in patients to enable the casualty crew to assess the extent of the impact. It's difficult to 'bring the scene' to the casualty staff. By the time the patient is brought into casualty he or she is cleaner, bandaged, bleeding has been stopped, and looks very different from what he or she looked like at the scene. The casualty staff don't see the height from which the person fell, or the various walls and objects the car hit as it rolled. All these things are important in a handover.

As a rule, after the patient has been packaged, the paramedic takes a close look at the car for comparison with the injuries sustained by the patient. We look for things like indentations in the windscreen; rotational forces on the seats; we look at the car seat – is it intact, turned, or bent? If the steering wheel is bent that gives one a good indication of what to expect with regard to chest injuries; did the dashboard stop the body, did the airbag deploy? Where are the skid marks? Is there a change in direction in the skid marks in relation to where the car came to land? Often there are other things in the car that give an indication of what went on; half-full beer bottles that are still ice cold, drugs, and so on. The most frightening thing, for me, is when you see a baby seat or baby paraphernalia and no sign of a baby.

The value of discovering what happened, or as we call it, 'the mechanism of injury', is of paramount importance at a scene in order to get a clear picture of what injuries to expect or look for. One Saturday night I was on duty in Eldorado Park. The call came in as a collapse. On my way there, I passed a motor accident scene. I started to slow down to investigate, as per protocol, and I noticed one of my colleagues in plain clothes approaching me. He told me all was well and gave me the thumbs-up. I carried on to the collapsed patient I'd been called out to.

I arrived at a park surrounded on four sides by houses. A woman reversing out of her driveway had spotted the young man lying on the ground in the park and called the ambulance. I looked at my patient; he was twenty something, trendy, good watch and shoes, no smell of alcohol, perfectly straight teeth, evidence of orthodontic work so I gathered he came from a reasonably well-to-do family. He smelled of a very nice aftershave; it was, after all, Saturday night and month end.

He had no doubt been on his way to a major *jol*[5]. I said 'had been' as he was clearly unconscious. I looked in his eyes; given his age, the problem could be drugs, but I found no evidence of this. There was no blood, no injury, no obvious trauma. I looked in his eyes again and noticed they were different. One was more dilated and sluggish when reacting to light, evidence that there was some degree of brain injury. The whole picture didn't fit. His pulse was dropping; the ambulance arrived and we were off to Baragwanath Hospital. En route my patient began to deteriorate rapidly.

Every piece of equipment was out and every dosage carefully calculated. My assistants kept pumping the chest hard. But I was baffled at the situation. Nothing was making sense and he was showing signs of coning. This is the last stage of a severe head injury, when the brain is so injured that it has swelled to the extent that it pushes against the path of least resistance. It will push behind the eyes, the nostrils,

---

5   Party

weeping blood out of the ears and nose as it continues to push out and finally down the spinal cord through the opening of the foramen magnum.

We worked on him non-stop. Rushing into casualty past loads of patients waiting to be seen, we continued to resus until we got to the resus bay. Then the doctors took over; he was lifted onto the resus table. ECG monitors were switched on, more drugs were drawn up, but I knew this was all academic; he was too far gone. I had no history on him, no mechanism of injury, nothing to give me an inkling about what was wrong with my patient. Mechanism of injury is a vital part of patient assessment.

I later found out that he was the driver of the vehicle that was involved in the accident I had passed on the way to my call. He had crashed the car, run four blocks, then collapsed in the park.

Had I known what had happened to the patient, I would have suspected trauma. Instead, I treated him as a medical patient initially because there was no reason to think otherwise. In this particular case, the patient's injuries were so severe that the outcome would likely have been the same, but in a less severe case the outcome might have been different.

Another call that illustrated the importance of knowing the mechanism of injury, was one that happened in Meredale; the call came in as a child having difficulty breathing. My heart skipped a beat. I drove extra fast – every minute counted against me. God spare this child, it's not right to take children away, especially not with breathing difficulty.

When I arrived I was confronted by a hysterical domestic worker pointing the way inside. The mother was trying to breathe into the child's mouth but she wasn't opening the airway enough, so her breaths were not effective. I took over, calming the mother down, at the same time trying to get a history. My crew hadn't arrived yet, so

I was being the octopus, grabbing equipment and doing CPR, asking for the history. Mom told me she was sitting in that chair, sewing; her child was playing near her, running around the chair. She suddenly started making strange sounds and collapsed. It sounded like a choking to me. Mom told me the child wasn't eating anything as she didn't allow sweets of any kind. Puzzled, I took out my laryngoscope and proceeded to open her airway. The vocal cords came into view and they were not closing completely as they should; they seemed to be stopping halfway. I took my Magills forceps, and the angel on my shoulder told me not to pass an endotracheal tube past the vocal cords, rather place the tip of the forceps just in front of the entrance to see if anything came out.

All of this was thought through in split seconds. I went ahead and almost missed it, a soft transparent jelly baby with its head bitten off and its shoulders jammed between the vocal cords. Yes, she did sneak a sweet from crèche into her pocket; Mom didn't know, so choking never featured as a mechanism of injury here. As long as I live, I will never forget that gasp as I removed the sweet and the child started to breathe, taking great big gulps of air. I remember physically shaking, and in my head all I could hear was myself saying thank you to the angel on my shoulder.

Of course, there is always the lighter side to arriving at a scene not knowing what the nature of the injury is or how it came about. I was dispatched one morning to the abattoir in City Deep knowing only that my patient had sustained an injury. What I did not know was that he had fallen sideways into one of the bloody furrows and twisted his ankle. When he tried to get up, he slipped again and by now was covered in blood from head to toe.

I arrived on the scene and asked where the patient was, only to see this apparition limping towards me. Every inch of his body was covered in blood. My heart skipped a few hectic beats; I could feel all reasoning going out the window. I must have missed this lecture –

where in heaven's name does one start? He must be leaking blood from all over, he must be like a sieve, I don't think I have enough bandages … all these thoughts went racing through my mind as I stared in utter stupefaction.

But not only was he dripping loads of blood – he was talking normally to another employee, only limping as he walked. He then proceeded to stop and take a phone call on his cell. I was rooted to the spot. I saw a man covered in blood, only his teeth were visible, speaking on the phone and clearly in no hurry to get himself treated. I felt the stirrings of hyperventilation about to run rampant in my own chest. With that amount of lost blood, surely he should be doing something like a death crawl, or one of those dying swan acts like in the old John Wayne movies? But no, completely unperturbed, smiling even, he continued chatting merrily …

* * *

3

The enigma of the bystanders

I AM convinced that the public watches too much television, and that there are way too many so-called medical programmes. In the same way as 'a little knowledge is a dangerous thing', so is that smattering of information, normally reserved for medical personnel, dangerous when bandied about by the general public. This excludes people suffering from Munchausen's Disease or Munchausen's-by-proxy – we will excuse them knowing, as we do, that they make it their life-time mission to learn the secret language of medicine.

These TV programmes are responsible for the general public at a scene arguing with a paramedic on the prognosis and diagnosis of a patient.

A fracture is a fracture – it's not an aneurism, or a thrombus, or any other Latin word the bystander has heard on Grey's Anatomy. Given the bystanders' paucity of grey matter, it gets especially interesting when they charge into the resuscitation bay, push past security and start telling the resuscitation team: "That man needs lidocaine". Does the sweet little gift from God even know what lidocaine is? What it's used for? How it's administered – do we give it intraocularly or intravenously? Who the lucky person is that should get it? What the contra indications are?

There is one group of bystanders who never let me down, who always bring a big smile to my face. They belong to that strange phenomenon in which individuals materialize out of the pavement cracks at the scene of an accident; in fact, they seem to ooze out of solid brick walls. I can be dispatched in the dead of night on a lonely road, far from civilization. It can be as quiet as an abandoned church, and yet within minutes of my arrival, they appear. Like the walking dead they slowly approach.

I once walked in a dense fog, torch in hand along a railway track, looking for a patient who was thrown out of a train. Not a single soul besides the train personnel walked next to me … but, sure enough, when I found my patient and began treatment, they materialized, these incredible things – the Bystanders. When did they begin to follow me? Is there a password? Or does the sound of a human body thudding to the ground set off a chain of events?

It begins with just a few arriving at the scene. But it's not long before they start to phone friends and colleagues to invite them to come and see. More cars pull up. More people. If it was day time this would surely be a great place for a food stand and a jumping castle.

But it doesn't stop there; no, it's not enough to keep them happy just identifying lost fingers in the long grass. They insist on actively inter-fering. Do you remember when you were at school? Every class had one. I'm not talking about the idiot, or the overachiever, or the fat guy, or the nymphomaniac – no, I'm talking about the one who thought he knew everything. The one who always had the answer even though he was wrong 90% of the time. But it didn't matter because he needed to be heard. He needed to fill all available airspace with his voice and know-it-all attitude. Ever wondered where those guys ended up? Wonder no more – for it's a certainty – they end up at my scene.

You spot them walking with purpose up to you; they do that once-over visual assessment of the patient while standing with their big feet on valuable equipment, and then They Speak.

"That man has a fracture," they will say with loud authority. Here I am, dealing with a seriously injured patient whose leg has been amputated in the accident and is lying some distance away. I am so tempted to come back with biting sarcasm; I want to say: "No, that's an extra leg", or the grateful approach: "Thank you for bringing that to my attention, I'm sure I would have missed his leg lying on the opposite side of the road." And right on cue, the smart aleck will proceed to tell everyone prepared to listen: "The patient is in shock." You would think I could figure out that the two litres of blood now soaking into the ground should be in his body.

And then there's the follow-up. After that particular bystander has told the medic the diagnosis and prognosis without the benefit of an X-ray, he will then hold court telling all around him about the time he himself sustained a fracture. He is really on a roll now. The only reason people stay and listen is that they think it gives them a legitimate excuse to be there.

After everyone has left, my colleagues and I joke about the cracks in the pavement. We jest about pulling up the pavement blocks to see what we will find underneath. Is there a whole city of one-figure-IQ folk who are small in size, like the oompalumpas from Charlie and the Chocolate Factory? And if they wafted up through the cracks and made contact with oxygen, would they become normal size, like they do in the story?

My favourite bystanders, however, have got to be the mothers who bring their children to the scene as if treating them to a visit to the zoo. These conscientious mothers carry their kids in their arms to see the blood. No amount of threatening or even police dogs will chase them away. They approach as if in a trance, almost hypnotized, walking purposefully towards you with steady concentration, staring intently like the cast from Night of the Living Dead.

* * *

While I was in Cape Town for a week doing an offshore survival course, I stayed with a very dear friend, Trevor. He had worked in the Johannesburg Ambulance Service before relocating to Cape Town. The course I was attending was held at night, so during the day I would do some calls with Trev. I had heard about the Cape Flats and how rough the majority of inhabitants are. Here, when you stop your response car, there is nothing quiet or subtle about how the bystanders approach you. You hear them from afar, like fog horns, beckoning all, bringing their own refreshments and their kids. They are not shy to ask you what happened, why, when, and what's going to happen now.

They are particularly astute at making loud, cheerful comments, "My broer, dis amper af"[6] to a half-comatose patient with badly fractured leg, sending him further into shock. This naturally brings out all the aspiring orthopaedic surgeons in the crowd who are only too happy to share their prognosis and much-needed diagnostic input. Sometimes you get a real gem who tells you he has a first-aid kit in his car.

When I worked in Soweto, I was stationed at Jabulani Fire Station. There was an area called Kersiedorp[7] that had a reputation for being really rough. It was a given that when an ambulance or response car

---

6   "My brother, it's nearly off"

7   "Candle Town" – so named as this was the last area to receive electricity

arrived at a scene, an elder of the community would come out with their *sjambok*[8] and stand by the car.

Heaven help anyone who tried to take any equipment; there would be swift repercussions from the elder. These areas house very poor people, people with soul, in whose faces are etched a multitude of life's disappointments, hardships and lost dreams. People who have very few material possessions, but who nevertheless are equipped for life by having a fantastic sense of humour.

The kids are fascinating; they always approach the car with a little sibling on their hip, hair in curlers and that wild look about them. Plus – an uninhibited vocabulary that would make a sailor blush.

It's not that they have the intention of stealing the equipment, it's just that when the response car with its bright lights and sirens approaches, they get so excited. It's a break from their mundane life of eating, sleeping and witnessing drunk parents hitting each other.

They approach the car in droves and one has to be a vigilant octopus as they pick up equipment from out of the boot, then turn around and walk off to show it to their friends. Their eyes light up as they recognize some of the equipment from TV shows and then begin, in their beautiful animated way, to tell the story about their emphysemic granny who needed oxygen. Why? Because she had turned purple like their mother's @#$% – no one says it with quite as much gusto as a coloured person.

* * *

---

8   A whip (also known as a *litupa*) 0.9 to 1.5 metres in length that tapers towards the tip

It was the Easter long weekend. This often proved to be as eventful as the Saturday Night Show and featured just as many players. It was always a good shift to work. Our first call was to a collapse at an old age home. We arrived there in Olympic record-breaking time to find the entire family plus neighbours sitting back, having tea and biscuits.

The body had been removed by the mortuary van four hours before. Bless the half-asleep cherub in the control centre who forgot to close the call on her screen. Great way to start the shift.

Happily this scenario is very rare! In fact, the control centre is another one of those areas we tend to forget about when we talk about ambulances and emergency services. This is step one, the first link in getting the right information, as quickly as possible, in order to get the right crew to whoever needs help. This can be a challenge when there is a language barrier. Far too many bystanders watch too much TV – as I've already told you. They see shows like E.R., 911 and Grey's Anatomy, and think they've picked up a qualification along the way.

This is also where they pick up big words like Unconscious. They know from having watched the TV that if you say the word 'unconscious,' then the serious stuff will happen. They won't send out the first-aiders, no sir! They will send out Johannesburg's finest; helicopters will be on standby and trauma surgeons will be answering pagers everywhere. But we are one step ahead of them. Not only have we seen the series also, we test them by asking them to do something for us. Something simple like, "Ask the patient when was the last time she drank anything with bubbles in it." And, right on cue, you hear the phone on their side being put down and they are having a conversation with an 'unconscious' person.

* * *

4

Casualty – theatre of the absurd

PATIENTS who come into casualty are just as entertaining as those on the road. The busy casualty where I do a lot of shifts is situated in an up-market middle-class area. The nurses' station faces the entrance – an ideal spot to take bets and guess what's wrong with the patient before he or she tells us.

Sometimes we are spot on, sometimes we are way off; like the time when, at just past three in the morning, a little cherub came in, slightly drunk, but nonetheless able to drive. He screeched his car to a halt outside and stumbled in. At the nurse's station the betting is on – speed of entrance, dishevelled look – there must be someone else in the car. As we get up to help, he delivers the punch line: "I want Viagra."

Behind me I hear sniggers, books closing and someone *sotto voce* says, "This should be good."

I approach him, maintaining as much composure as possible, while at the same time trying to sneak a look into the car to see if the other half is just as desperate that he gets his medication. I explain this is not a pharmacy, but if he still wants Viagra he will need to see a doctor who will prescribe it. He begins to swear at me and his obnoxious behaviour is now bordering on assault. I tell him to go down to the pharmacy; maybe they will alleviate his flaccid problem. He storms off amidst a cloud of profanities. We quickly phone the pharmacist and warn him of the forthcoming attraction and give him time to mobilize security to remove him. No one wins any bets that time.

At the same casualty on another occasion, I watched a patient pull up on his motor bike, dismount slowly and start walking towards the registration desk. I reckoned there was no serious injury as he was still walking, albeit slowly. Then the punch line: "Good morning, I need to see a surgeon as I have a large object embedded in my rectum." Again, no bets were won.

Speaking of which … a certain Mr A made an impression that had us talking for months. I was still a student at the time and, unbeknown to me, he was not a stranger to the casualty section. I entered the cubicle to find him lying on the bed. A quick glance revealed he was in his late fifties, dirty and unkempt, although he was wearing good shoes, also an expensive watch … perhaps he was gardening and didn't live in this area. Did I mention that, apart from loving my job, I'm also a frustrated profiler?

There was no obvious bleeding that I could see. I proceeded to take his vital signs and when finished I asked him to give me the reason he'd come to casualty. He replied that he would rather not say. I thought this odd as he was not drunk or aggressive and, strangely enough, he was very cooperative apart from not wanting to give me a history of his affliction. I did notice, however, that there were no other medical personnel in casualty.

On closer inspection, I saw that the patient's fingernails were surrounded by blood but there were no associated cuts or injuries to his hands. I closed the cubicle curtain and went to call a doctor. I found everyone in the restroom with the door closed, laughing loudly. Doing everything by the book because I can be anal, I dutifully handed over to the first person who managed to stop laughing. I still did not realize they were laughing at me.

While this was taking place the ambulance service brought in a man with a gunshot wound to his head and we bolted out of the room to assist. Mr A was relegated to second place.

After the 'gunshot head' had been stabilised, I ventured out of the resuscitation bay towards the cubicle where Mr A was, and noticed the curtains were still drawn. I wanted to make sure he was okay and to reassure him that we hadn't forgotten about him. I pulled the curtain back and did a double take. There was Mr A on his back holding his ankles like a woman in labour. One of the doctors had his hands knuckle deep in Mr A's rectum and was tugging on what I found out later was an orange.

The doctor clearly was not winning; the exertion had made him red faced and the veins in his neck were standing out alarmingly. I thought he was about to burst an aneurism. One leg was on the bed while the other was gripping the floor with his running shoe, much like a pool player poised for a difficult shot. A second doctor suggested they send for the obstetrician to borrow a delivery forceps as the doctor working in and around Mr A's rectum could literally not get a grip. The forceps arrived and left. Some more consultants arrived, discussed the matter, and left. An orthopaedic surgeon decided to use a device that resembled a corkscrew, managing only to remove a small piece of the orange, shaped in a perfectly round circle ... much like a melon scoop for a fruit sundae.

While all this was happening new patients were arriving. Still we remained hard at work with the 'embedded orange emergency'. Then a bright spark suggested giving the patient more muscle relaxant. I'm not sure why – his rectum at this stage was so wide you could fit a coke can in it – but it seemed to work.

The most amazing thing is that throughout this mammoth procedure, Mr A had no expression on his face whatsoever. He lay like a veteran expectant mother, still holding his ankles and looking as if about to give birth. The tugging, pulling and strategizing that went on were constant and innovative, to say the least. And his version of how the orange got there? He fell on it!

One night shift in casualty, a patient came in just after midnight. His story was that he had not slept a wink for three days. I knew that the doctor had just done a 24-hour shift at Baragwanath and was extremely tired. Instead of waking her, I suggested things that the patient could do to fall asleep – natural things, like drink warm milk, count sheep, peel an apple slowly, read the yellow pages, do breathing exercises, watch the Parliamentary channel, but he was adamant he needed to see the doctor. After exhausting my ideas on how to get him to relax and sleep, I went with a heavy heart to wake the doctor. I spent ten minutes behind the door explaining, "Yes, I kid you not, he can't sleep … needs to see you. Yes, I have tried everything. No, I have not assaulted him. Yes, I am positive we don't have an electric chair in casualty."

The exhausted doctor finally emerged, dishevelled and red-eyed. Together we walked to the waiting room, only to find our little ray of sunshine fast asleep, snoring very loudly, mouth open, as if waiting for a dental mirror to be inserted.

I flew with Annie on the Emergency helicopter for four years; she was the chief flight sister. She was one of those people with whom you felt completely safe. A bit like being in a dangerous situation and knowing because you have one of Charlie's Angels at your side, nothing bad can possibly happen to you. Or, being like a cartoon character, you can be shot or smacked unconscious and you know you'll get up again because Annie is with you. I trust her with my life.

So there we were one night working at Johannesburg casualty, my good friend on duty with me. Casualty is rocking, it's month end and people are spending their money on alcohol, and lots of it.

In walks a critter, a real gangster type, with blood all over his torn clothes. He is grinning from ear to ear and has obviously mixed his alcohol with the organic weed, or something just as potent. Annie and I are really tired; it's been a busy shift, there are not enough beds, and the waiting-room seats are all occupied. It looks like a scene from a Quentin Tarantino movie. He walks up to us, looks Annie straight in the eye and says, "I'm a gangster piece of shit." Annie gives him the once-over optical assessment and answers: "So what do you want me to do about that?"

"You must treat me like a gangster piece of shit," he says, dispersing alcohol fumes with every word. She looks him straight in the eye. "Well, gangster piece of shit, @#$%! off out of my emergency room."

I hold my breath. I'm thinking, okay, maybe she's lost all sense of fear – must be the government coffee. No need, he turns around and walks straight back out through the doors. There is a long pregnant pause as we await his return. Nothing happens. To this day we often joke about him; maybe he'll come back one day to have that bleeding stopped.

And then there are the regulars, like Mr W who comes in for free tea, sandwiches and a bath because years ago he very altruistically helped the hospital manager change a flat tyre on his way to work. And Mrs S who takes off all her clothes to have the doctor examine her sore throat – and insists on having a male doctor. And finally there's poor Mr T who will only allow brunette sisters to insert catheters or help him in any way.

One of my favourite standard replies comes when I'm taking a history. I'll ask the patient what medication she is on and she'll confidently reply: "Those little yellow pills in the morning and the white ones at night."

And how could we get by without those old folk who tell you they went through the Great Depression and don't see the need to pay full price for the treatment received now?

* * *

Something that manages to drive me and most other casualty workers right up the wall and down the other side, is people who have no idea what an emergency is and demand to be pushed up the list to a priority position. It always plays out like an episode out of South Park.

At 3 am in walks a patient with an 'emergency' case of athlete's foot. In a busy casualty overflowing with urgent cases, something inside snaps and I'm tempted to say, "You, sir, have come in with – what? A little flaking between your toes? Oh, do sit down before you pass out … this is a grave matter. Let me take your vitals. Goodness, we are bordering on decompensate shock. Wait … let me set up a drip … a drip for a drip. I'm afraid I'll have to prescribe bedrest, preferably in a dark room, no noise, and chicken soup … better still, let me put aside *all* my other work to attend to this most life-threatening of illnesses. I will supersede all chains of command and go right to the top; I will urgently fax a demand that your athlete's foot gets code red status, that we have a helicopter ready for a hot onload, and that no other patients may take up any of my time for the rest of the day. Lie down; let me attend to these offensive bits of dried skin caused by you not drying between your toes. Explain to me – why has this now become *my* problem …?" But I don't say any of this. I attend to him as it is clearly bothering him.

Believe it or not, our busiest day in casualty is a Sunday during the day shift. I am certain that these visitors are lonely, bored people with no family or friends, who have a to-do checklist that has written, at the very top, **Sunday: Visit Casualty**. They come in and sit patiently, sometimes for up to an hour. You escort them into the cubicle and start your patient history. "Why did you come to visit us today, sir?" You notice no cough, no plaster or bandage, no limping, and no scratching. He then delivers the punch line: "Well, I've had this headache for about four months now, and I thought I should have it seen to." My knuckles are white as I write down his main complaint. I maintain composure. I want to tell him there and then, "No sir, you're just lonely, there's nothing interesting on TV, you had nothing better to do, so you came here for some company and don't mind paying a casualty fee." But I don't say these things. I carry on my assessment and take vital signs.

Cross-cultural emergencies

It takes a true, born-and-bred South African to appreciate the African vernacular, which is a mixture of English, Afrikaans and township lingo, almost like the new *Fanagalo*. *Fanagalo* is the language spoken on the mines; it's a mixture of English, Afrikaans and a bit of all the different black tribal languages of the people who work there. If you can speak *Fanagalo*, then you are guaranteed renewed respect from your black colleagues as you will be understood in any province of this beautiful country of ours. Having said this, I remember situations where *Fanagalo* wasn't needed – the person said it just like it was.

On one occasion, Sister Fine and I were sent to a certain ward in a hospital. Our mission was to collect a patient and take him to another hospital. We had to 'package' him for a helicopter flight. Normally, there is a degree of activity surrounding a patient about to leave his bed to fly in a helicopter, but when we arrived at the ward, it was all quiet. Actually there was nothing happening at all.

Everything looked normal: patients fast asleep; sisters passed out on counter tables; cleaner cleaning the floors; TV channel stuck on test pattern. Sister Fine and I were intrigued.

We woke the sister on duty up, after wiping her dribble. She looked at us as if we were insane – couldn't we see she was napping? We informed her in a most irritated way that we were there to pick up so-and-so for his flight. She looked at us and said, "Oh no, that patient she demised."

We were at a loss, looking like utter fools.

"What?" asked Annie, "What time did he demise, Sister?"

She was on a roll now; full of self-importance, she grabbed some papers on the desk, flipped through them and in her most authoritarian voice said: "Patient's last gasp was at ten o'clock."

* * *

All of us do it at some time or another when we are together and in uniform – we go into victim mode. There is just so much to complain about, and how, given the chance, we would run the ambulance service, blah, blah, blah. And with this in mind I remember the following incident.

In every field one works in, there are little gimmicks or things one does to make oneself remember important information or events. In emergency medicine we have the Glasgow Coma Scale. It is a method of determining if the patient's neurological fallout is improving or deteriorating based on three aspects: eye response, response to pain, and verbal response. It is measured at regular intervals to give us an indication of what we are dealing with. It is used world-wide and every person who is trained in emergency medicine knows this scale by heart. Whether working on the road or in casualty, we are able to calculate it in seconds.

I arrived at a hospital once to fetch a patient and there was a highly qualified sister attending to him. How did I know she was highly qualified? Well, she had all four stripes in multi-colour on her epaulettes, which meant she was not a mere nurse but a sister who had specialized in community nursing (yellow), midwifery (green), and psychiatry (blue).

Said sister was next to the patient, ready to do her handover. Now, we all know how understaffed the health services in our country are, how the budget is squandered, and so on. So when I asked what the patient's Glasgow Coma Scale was, she replied on cue, "Well, you know how it is; this hospital is a small one, there's no money put aside to buy one."

* * *

Sometimes, it may sound funny to an outsider, but the language barrier causes frustration on all sides. And if there's a life-threatening situation about to unravel, it can be serious.

The following is a transcript of a real conversation to a hospital, asking for help.

CALLER: Please help. Somebody, she has been bitten by the car.

CALL TAKER: Do you mean she has been run over by a car?

CALLER: No she has been bitten, she was standing by the road, doing nothing, next, the car she comes and bitten the woman.

CALL TAKER: Where did the car bite her, sir?

CALLER: Here, in Mofolo North.

CALL TAKER: No sir, where on the body did the car bite her?
Silence.

CALL TAKER: Sir, the car that has bitten her, where is it?

CALLER: *Hai wenna*[9], that car she run away.

CALL TAKER: Sir, are you saying the car is not there anymore?

CALLER: Yes, that is what I am saying, she has bitten the woman and then she *voetsek*[10].

CALL TAKER: Sir, where are you, what is your address?

CALLER: I am here, next to the *spaza*[11], by the left side of the road.

CALL TAKER: Sir, I need an address. Where is this *spaza* shop?

CALLER: Hey (profanities in an African language) I am here by the *spaza* shop, everybody knows it, ask anybody.

CALL TAKER: Sir, I need a proper address, the ambulance doesn't know where you are.

CALLER: Just tell them the *spaza* here by the road, in Mofolo North, very near the garage.

CALL TAKER: Sir, do you see a street name anywhere near you?

CALLER: (More profanities) No, I don't see words for the road, because everybody knows where the *spaza* shop here is in Mofolo North …

And believe me, this type of conversation happens regularly.

* * *

---

9 An expression of surprise, wonder or frustration

10 Went away

11 An informal general store

5

People are living there

WORKING twelve-hour shifts, most of them being in a car, one needs to be very comfortable in that small space. My response car became so much a second home to me that I would savour the familiar smells and the welcoming feel of my special cushion. The cushion has always been a joke amongst my colleagues when we're on shifts. I'm not exactly the world's tallest woman – being a proud five footer. I get a better perspective on the world sitting on a cushion or a folded blanket, and when I was a station officer at Central fire station, there would always be a blanket set aside especially for my short arse, if you'll excuse the expression.

Hour upon hour in my car has changed me. I can fall asleep bent like a pretzel while listening to the radio; I've learnt to drive at high speeds while eating, talking on the radio and looking up a street in a map book all at the same time. And did I forget to mention also changing the radio station when a Dolly Parton number comes on?

As an incurable insomniac I prefer working the night shifts. There is something very magical about watching the sun rise on a city that you have spent the last twelve hours courting – moving deep inside her, getting to know her secret little roads and broken fences; the not-so-secret places where the ladies of the night take their steamers; the entrances to elegant buildings where the street children sleep; the park benches under the beautiful trees in Joubert Park where the down-and-outs lay their heads for the night; the top all-night establishments that serve the best coffee.

There are probably very few jobs that have the kaleidoscopic inter-mingling of humanity that mine has. One moment I'll be on call in Sandton and the next I'll be witness to the dregs of humanity housed in buildings so derelict one can't believe anyone would want to occupy them. Shades of Athol Fugard's *People Are Living There*. One can acknowledge the triumph of suburbs that have been brought back to life by young money and new initiative; while cheek-by-jowl with them are suburbs so run down, so overrun by drug lords, that the rot is indistinguishable from the occupants.

One gets to know the city smells and her humours. Like the families who insist on having their couches on the front lawn and see no reason to put them back inside. There are also those 'aesthetically pleasing' suburbs where all the inhabitants have cars on the pavement in various stages of being dismantled or stolen, whichever way you want to look at it.

On the positive side, there are the churches in the city centre that offer refuge to the many vagrants who have given up hope; people who once had families but have been forgotten except by the parish. Or the familiar, abandoned building entrances that offer shelter to those who have a mattress to lie down on for the night. The street children sleep bundled up in newspapers and plastic sheeting in the doorways and entrances of the filthy buildings that once stood grand and proud against the city skyline.

The Hillbrow skyline is to Joburgers what Table Mountain is to the Capetonians and what the Colosseum was to the Romans.

There is currently a big movement afoot to revive and revamp the city centre. There are amazing edifices like the Franklin, which wouldn't look out of place next to the Trump Towers. But they are surrounded by buildings that are run down and not safe to occupy; it makes for such a dichotomy and is so fascinating.

In its day, Hillbrow was a melting pot of different cultures, mostly European. It was a very 'happening' place – the bars, discos and all-night coffee bars where memories were made, interesting people were introduced to one another and much learning about other cultures was done in a non-threatening way.

I used to live in Hillbrow many years ago, twenty years back. I, like so many of my generation, either lived in a commune, shared a flat or, if you had a really good job, rented your own flat. One could walk alone late at night to the Look & Listen record shop where the records flowed out onto the pavement and the people working there always knew where to find anything you requested. You could stop and have an ice cream at the Norgenvas right next to the Wurstbudder where they made the world's best coffee; this is where I first tasted filter coffee and evaporated milk.

Treading lightly down memory lane, I am a child again and I vividly recall the lights and beautiful Christmas decorations in Joubert Park; it was traditional to be taken by one's parents to the city centre to see the display of rainbow-coloured lights – thank you, Eskom. These were strung up along all the main streets. I very nostalgically remember the sight and smell of the amazing flowers on display at the indoor plant hothouse in the Park; and adjacent to this you could watch the clever people playing chess on a huge chessboard on the ground.

There was always a good act to catch at the Chelsea Hotel such as E-void or, for the more refined, off to the Black Sun to watch greats like Thandi Claasen, Jennifer Ferguson, Amanda Strydom and the fascinating Baroness. You knew you were with the in-crowd as all those artists went on to No 58 the following month where you'd have a pre-booked table. They were the most fabulous dens of iniquity and talent, and quite the most memorable *jol* any one could experience.

If you're the right age, I'm sure you remember Bella Napoli and the ever-popular disco Boobs; and around the corner for people batting for the other side, Connections in Pretoria Street and further down, the Butterfly Bar (now Skyline). When you had tired yourselves out on the dance floor, you all walked to Fontana for a fresh bag of rolls and their delectable roast chickens. Then you positioned your posteriors right there on the pavement outside, and ate with your fingers while you watched the jolly Saturday Night Show walk by.

There was Milky Lane and no fewer than three Porterhouse steak-houses for that beginning-of-the-month meal when you felt rich.

On Sunday mornings you met your friends for breakfast at the Wimpy opposite the Reg Park gym and watched the nutters sweating it out while you stuffed your face; and later, if you had any space left, you remembered Bimbo's for great hamburgers. Then on the way home, you picked up a cake or chelsea buns from the San Marco bakery … Did people have weight problems in those days, I wonder?

And lastly, let's not forget the Casablanca Roadhouse where I could never figure out how they managed to drive a World War Two tank onto the verge and leave it there. Their Smartie cups (ice cream full of wickedly-coloured chocolate drops, for the uninitiated), were legendary and the nursing sisters at the Joburg Gen would always bribe the paramedics to treat them to at least two per night shift.

And while we're onto reminiscing, what about the Ponte building, that huge round tower-like edifice that can be seen for miles around on a clear Highveld night? It used to carry the Coca-Cola sign and now it touts for Vodacom. When you are flying by helicopter at night and coming from the east, it looms in the distance like a beacon, a lighthouse in a sea of concrete, a bit like the Statue of Liberty must have been to all those ships that brought in the hopeful immigrants to the bountiful shores of America.

The Ponte was a very sought-after address in its heyday. With more than thirty storeys and a most spectacular view, what more could anyone ask? Sadly, however, it has deteriorated along with the rest of the slum-like buildings that now characterise Hillbrow. There is rarely a day when one of the lifts even works in this building, and when they do, they only go up to the 18th floor.

And sadder still, the nature of the occupants reflects the lethargy of the whole place. Everyone is concerned only for number one, and even though it's very obvious from my uniform that I work for emergency services, they will still block the lift or make sure it stops on every floor. The possibility that there could be someone in dire need of emergency treatment either doesn't occur to them or doesn't bother them much. I make it very obvious that I'm in a hurry, I am carrying a *katunda*[12] of equipment, but they remain selfishly unperturbed. However, let the tables be turned – believe me, they will be the ones making the loudest noise about having waited so long for an ambulance.

The Ponte's architecture was way ahead of its time. The architects had the foresight to build a café, laundromat and other services on the ground floor for use by the inhabitants. It was designed, much like Standard Bank City, as a self-contained entity, which meant that people living there had no reason to go outside it, except obviously to work.

---

12 A large amount

Hillbrow, what a place! I'm sure it's a name known to people in other countries too. Foreign tourists are warned not to go there except in groups, and never at night. But in its heyday it was an incredible social melting pot. There was a large population of people from Europe and the Middle East – Greek, Italian and Jewish communities flourished there. Kosher food was readily available. Sadly it now resembles nothing more than an old woman who refuses to give up the grandiloquence of the past. Here and there are signs of the remnants of white people who have tried to escape the inner city and Nigerian overrun blocks that sell a steady supply of drugs, which come from as far afield as Bolivia. The sadly dilapidated buildings, tiny neglected gardens, and peeling paint bear testimony to the ground zero fall of the inner-city cosmopolitan way of life, the epicentre where the amicable cohabitation of blacks and whites came crashing down. It's just a ghetto now.

※ ※ ※

Tucked away in odd corners are places that we drive past every day without ever realizing that real flesh-and-blood people actually live there. They are usually the places that one would rather forget; places that are so deceptive in their appearance that it would never enter your mind that people could live and breathe and have their being there.

I've tried to describe a good call, but the true definition is difficult to verbalise. Anyone who has ever been high on drugs would recognize the feeling, except that with a good call there are only good after-effects – and they last longer. A good call is real and raw; it lingers in the labyrinths of your mind to be replayed when you get nostalgic or need to call on resources to answer questions. Or you just let the aftermath sit inside you, occupying a special place, restoring your faith in humanity and giving you a new perspective on life …

A very humbling call I clearly remember happened on a Sunday many years ago just before lunch. I had had a few calls earlier, but now it was getting quiet as it always does before the midday meal.

I had parked my car under a tree opposite the cheetah enclosure at the Johannesburg Zoo, one of my favourite places. I enjoyed the absolute contrast between the wild creature I was watching and some of the wild creatures I have to treat.

Then I receive the call – it is a collapse.

I start the car and scream off to the destination. I am familiar with the area; I have been driving these roads for more than eleven years. It is in an industrial area, bleak, grey, steel and concrete everywhere like grey grass growing. I arrive at the address but all I see is a long wall that spans two blocks and houses a scrapyard. I radio back and ask to confirm the address and proceed to do a u-turn – I still don't see anything. I'm not sure if it's the Italian in me, or just my impatient nature, but I start to get irritated.

The control centre radios back that they are having problems phoning back as the call came from a public call box. I drive around the block and toot my siren again. More than twelve minutes have been wasted waiting; I am about to drive away when I glance in my rear view mirror and see an old man walking very slowly and purposefully toward me. He is poorly dressed, thin and gesticulating wildly. The image of a human windmill comes to mind. A range of emotions floods me, first relief that I have found him, which is replaced by anger as he has clearly not collapsed. Next comes the trepidation that he is not the patient. All these emotions play themselves along my neurons in a matter of split seconds. I lean out and ask him if he called for the ambulance. He confirms this in broken English.

I place my jump bag on my back, feeling much like a tortoise, grab the cardiac monitor and the oxygen cylinder and follow him. As we walk I try to get a patient history but this is not exactly successful as we have a serious language barrier, to put it mildly.

We continue walking through the scrapyard towards the back of the premises. We pass rows of old, broken cars; some neatly stacked, others thrown carelessly on top of one another. It's reminiscent of those horrible documentaries about the Second World War – how they tossed dead prisoners onto a pile waiting to be buried.

The smell of rusted metal assails my nostrils and there are puddles of water everywhere because it rained the day before. I notice a few thin and neglected feral cats and wonder how they survive here. My equipment is getting heavy and I don't see any life other than the two of us and the mangy-looking cats. At the back of the yard against a wall are four run-down double-decker buses; they have no wheels, and all the windows have been boarded up with make-shift material.

Ironically, on the side of one is an advert about a wonderful product, which, if you imbibe it, will ensure that you can conquer the world. As often as I say nothing surprises me any more, this situation clearly does. There are people living here! This is their home. This is where they come to rest at night, where they invite their friends, where they feel safe. This is where they seek refuge, and this is where I see pictures of their soccer heroes on the 'wall' inside. This place that people drive past every day, completely oblivious to the fact that there is life here right alongside huge metal piles of cars.

It's a secret place where no post will ever be delivered, no phone will ring, no electricity supplied to make life more comfortable. I notice that there are little objects that define the people who live here; photos on the wall, of family members with big smiles, taken right here at the scrapyard. An odd assortment of crockery is used as it is, stained, chipped and skew, but it's their crockery, it tells a story of its own. I wonder about all those meagre meals, prepared nonetheless by willing hands, bearing testimony to human dignity.

I examine the patient, an old woman who is very weak, barely conscious. I take her vitals, place her on an intravenous drip and administer some dextrose. A few minutes go by. While I wait for the dextrose to enter her bloodstream, I busy myself with putting equipment away. She slowly becomes conscious and aware; the relief on the watching faces is almost palpable. The old man in his broken English thanks me, he asks God to bless me, his handshake is enough to loosen my dental fillings. He thinks I am wonderful but I feel anything but wonderful. I look back and remember with shame how impatient I was; I feel ashamed that I worry about what I will be serving for dessert on Friday night. The crisis they were facing has trivialized what so many people consider a worry, that I feel – no other word for it – shamed.

I see the look in the eyes of the little ones as they stare at me in my uniform, with eager curiosity but also fear. Apart from my flight suit, my everyday uniform is very similar to a policeman's, with lots of badges and important-looking decorations. I register the fear in their eyes. I would love to let them hear their heartbeat with my stethoscope – it's always a great ice breaker. But how do you do this when there is a language barrier, when they shrink away from you like sensitive sea anemones?

It's always an unforgettable moment for me to watch the expression on a child's face the first time they hear their own heart beat. They have been taught about their heart – seen pictures of it in books, seen it bleed when the guy on television is shot in the chest, maybe even eaten it – but never heard its beautiful rhythm.

How do you begin to say: *I don't know why you and I are here in this lifetime on earth; why I have what I have and you don't; why I am this colour and you are another; why I am a young woman and you are a child or an old man.*

These moments are so intimate, so unrehearsed, so raw and real, it's an aspect of my job I would not give up for anything; it makes me feel alive, makes me dream both small and huge dreams. These are moments shared between only me and a patient, and no one else; like the many babies I have delivered, handing the squealing bundle to the fragile new mother. One cannot forget the look in her eyes or the singing of the elders in the community that makes my hair stand straight up.

It's a very emotive job; one can't be indifferent about it. There are so many feelings that come with it, like the goose-bumps I get when the sisters at Baragwanath spontaneously break into song at the hospital bed after the death of a child; the feeling of a patient's sweaty hand; the roughness of an old person's arthritic fingers holding mine, or the desperate way they hang on as you assist them up stairs; the warmth of a patient's blood as I apply a bandage; the joy in the moment when one feels the incredible strength in the way a newborn grasps your fingers; the smile after a patient's stressed breathing is relieved; the abatement of fear on a mother's face when she hears the words: "Your baby will be fine now."

And there are many sad sounds, the outward expression of pain and suffering – like fractured ribs rubbing against the inside wall deep in the chest cavity or the desperate wheezing of an asthmatic, like a fish out of water; and the worst – the rasping sound deep inside a patient's lungs as he takes his last few breaths on this earth. And the opposite – the heart-stopping first cry a brand-new, just-born baby makes when you have brought it out into the light and independence. These are split-second moments in time that you cannot explain to another person without feeling that there is so much more to say.

These moments and memories are crystal clear in my mind.

* * *

Sometimes I have seen a side to human beings that I find hard to fathom, almost incomprehensible. I remember answering a call in a fairly affluent area of Johannesburg.

The call came in as an overdose. After you have been doing this for as long as I have, you get to be wise, more than street-wise. You develop an intuition and wisdom that enable you to cope with this job. You have the sort of wisdom a profiler needs to study humans and understand from their behaviour what makes them do certain things. It's a wisdom you will never find in self-help books, an understanding that is learned only from closely observing humans at their most vulnerable and emotionally raw. It's a bit like a psychotherapist but in reality, almost like deconstructing the human frontal lobe.

An overdose in an affluent area makes you sit up and take notice. In these suburbs the people who take drugs have been doing it for years, in what they probably see as a 'civilized' way. There is lots of money around; children know this from a young age, and are groomed to carry on the family name and traditions. So the taking of hard drugs like heroin isn't commonplace; these young people are into the designer drugs, which everyone does at closed parties amongst friends.

They get elegantly wasted in sitting rooms that are wall-to-wall Biggie Best, and snort lines on imported marble tops in kitchens that have coffee machines that cost more than my entire car sound system. They don't usually mainline as this would ruin their beautiful bodies, those pampered forms they drag to the gym every day and keep trim by dancing for twenty hours at raves, fuelled on Ecstasy.

These are people who regularly make the back pages of magazines like *Condé Nast* and *Style*. Their regular supplier doesn't hang around on street corners waiting for a code word to be whispered. No, here Mohammed goes to the mountain (no race implication intended), or they arrange to meet the supplier in a parking lot. The money and the drugs are thrown out of one car window and into the other simultaneously. A passer-by who is unaware would completely miss the smooth little transaction that just went down in the parking lot of the up-market MacDonald's.

The occasional coke overdose is normally not intentional. The scene is usually the same: worried friends who have sobered up very quickly meet you at the door with shocked faces. They do not look you in the eye, but go scurrying past, practically leopard crawling. No one ever knows how much coke he did, no one ever knows where it came from, details are always very sketchy. If the party is very big then most of the people present won't even know the victim.

On this particular day, I arrive and make my way through the topiary in a garden that looks like an Edward Scissorhand's set – a beautiful, manicured garden and a house that clearly shows money isn't an object. I am always fascinated by the fact that wealthy people have houses that are perfect; there is precision attached to every little thing, total attention to detail.

Their tables are always dusted, the glass always shines, and there are never those pieces of folded brown paper tucked under the legs to keep them level. I never see ugly wires hanging from their computers or surround sound. The cars in the driveway are always new; they look as if they've just this minute come back from the car-wash. The registration plates are usually personalized.

Even the animals are gorgeous, well-groomed, pedigreed specimens – no pavement specials residing here – absolutely no mixing of these carefully managed gene pools. Everything works in these houses except the headspace of the owners.

I am greeted by a manservant, a butler no less on this early morning. The kitchen is Provence-meets-big-wallet, wall-to-wall glass inlaid with soft backdrop lighting, chunky real wood, no lamination, and naturally, there are matching plug covers. My patient is a young man, twenty-something, designer labels from watch to shoes. He is not unconscious; he is dead. I recheck pulse, cardiac function, pupil response. The butler, who lives over the garage, tells me he heard him leave last night but didn't hear him coming in again.

I hear voices in the adjacent room and prepare myself to tell them the awful news. The mother enters the kitchen; I know it's the mother because there's a strong family likeness. She is very regal-looking. What perturbs me is she doesn't even glance at the body. She glances at her espresso machine, then turns to me and asks when I am going to remove the body!!!!

I presume she is in shock so I give her time to think about what she has said. I know any minute now the wave of realization will hit her. The realization that from this day forth her son will be spoken about in the past tense, relegated to the past, from an *is* to a *was*. There will be no family photos of him taken ever again; from this day on there is a date at the end of that hyphen when they speak about him.

I am totally focused, waiting for her composure to collapse, but it doesn't happen. She asks again: when will I remove the body? I explain I am not allowed to remove it – it's a crime scene. As it is an unnatural death the police will be here to photograph the body and take statements.

She is staring straight through me and I find it unnerving. I'm the Scorpio, that's *my* trick; she is very controlled and asks once more when I will remove the body. I look for those tell-tale signs of the beginning of the realization of the loss – the wringing of the hands, the pushing back of the cuticles, those little distractions that seem to make it all better for a few agonizing seconds. But they are not there, not an iota of evidence that she feels anything.

Instead she becomes very edgy, asking all sorts of questions pertaining to the removal of the body, despite my having said we were not authorized to do so. I hear her ask my colleagues: Who is in charge here? They tell her that I am the most senior, and reiterate that the body cannot be removed. Then comes the unbelievable punchline. The lady informs us in a most irritated manner that she has things to do; there are caterers coming at ten.

I told you – everything works here except the headspace.

* * *

When I started my career, there were a lot of Welconal (pinks) cases in Hillbrow. You could spot the junkies a mile off, always thin, haggard, wearing a thick jacket or jersey in summer, pinpoint pupils and missing teeth. The pharmacies in Hillbrow were forever being broken into and script pads would go missing from doctors' consulting rooms. They would even break into the old age homes where many of the terminal patients were on Welconal because it is a powerful analgesic and was prescribed for patients with terminal cancer.

There are a number of sleazy hotels in Hillbrow where the dregs of humanity live. Once I was called to an overdose in one such hotel. An addict had spiked up and was so high that he passed out sitting on the toilet, with his feet braced against the door.

I climbed over the cubicle wall and was able to reach him and open his airway, which had closed off. There was no time to undo his jacket in that small space so I elected to cut his jacket so that I could inject him with a reversal agent. Welconal, like any analgesic, will drop blood pressure but more importantly, it suppresses the central nervous system thereby slowing down, or worse, stopping the patient's breathing. We managed to get him out, onto a scoop, and into the ambulance.

On the way to the hospital he began to wake up and started to scratch his face until it bled; he could see spiders crawling all over him. I realized that no amount of calm talking would convince him there were no arachnids in sight.

When we arrived, we wheeled him into medical casualty and handed over to the doctor on duty. With my back turned to him, I heard him suddenly start to scream and swear at me for cutting his leather jacket. I ignored him and kept walking to my ambulance. Out of the corner of my eye I saw a security guard hurtling towards me; he pushed me to the ground just as I heard that unmistakable sound of an oxygen bottle missing my head by inches. This grateful sod was running behind me and had taken a swipe at me, but thankfully I was saved by the security guard. Who says there are no angels out there?

* * *

Have you ever noticed how the Eastern side of the Joburg map seems to breed odd people? Whenever there is a story that is amazing – the kind you only read about in a *You* magazine exposé, like satanic cults, paedophile nursery school teachers parading as dedicated educators, women genuinely in love with their great uncles, people who keep their dearly departed's remains in a coolroom under the house and so on – have you ever noticed how many come from Kempton Park, Benoni, or Brakpan? A call I went on took place in the same town that the one good thing – our very own home-grown Charlize Theron – hails from.

A Benoni barnacle had managed to acquire a limpet mine. He decided in his brandy-and-coke-induced state that he would walk up to the automatic teller machine, open the deposit box, place the limpet mine in it and wait for the machine to spew forth. Who needs Gold Reef City?

All went according to plan except for a minor flaw in his strategy. He must have stood too long in front of the machine because it blew up in his face, making an almighty noise and waking up half the town. While he lay on the ground with 40% burns, his fellow citizens were making like the people in the Bible. Halleluja! Manna was falling from heaven and this was the best get-rich-quick scheme they'd ever seen! As we landed in the helicopter, we managed to scatter more bank notes with the turbulence, causing even greater jubilation amongst the gatherers and much sweating on the part of the pilot who was finding it difficult to land. Nevertheless, the one-armed bandit was flown to hospital and faced charges when he was discharged. Talk about adding insult to injury.

* * *

Johannesburg train station is like all train stations – huge. This means that, when one is called there, the medics have to walk a fair distance to find the patient. Generally speaking, and taking Murphy into account, patients are very inconsiderate. They always live on the top floor where the lifts don't work; weigh a ton; have accidents during peak hours; have more accidents when it's cold and wet; and their guts are always full of food and beer, which gets deposited on my shoes. And at a train station – yes, it's always the last platform.

The call came in that a woman had thrown herself in front of a train. My cerebral cortex was trying to figure out why I had been called to this; there can't be too much one can do for her. After schlepping equipment for about a hundred platforms and back and not finding a patient, frustration started setting in. But I did find a little cherub in a proudly South African Railways uniform and asked him if he knew anything about the patient. His face lit up – Bingo, he did! He pointed out a woman lying on a bench that I had passed two platforms back. She had indeed thrown herself in front of the train – but the train was standing still.

* * *

6

The very young and the very old

THERE is one sure factor that separates lesser paramedics from the top paramedics – how they deal with children. You either do kids' calls or you avoid them like the plague and tell everyone on the mike that you're "still very busy with your current call." I suppose working with children is much like a vet's job – your patient can't always articulate the location, degree or type of pain they're feeling. So treating them takes immense patience and the ability to cut yourself off from their screams as you assess the situation and determine the exact problem.

But nothing is as distressing to me as a child who cries incessantly. I can handle a phone that rings for minutes on end, when clearly the person on the other side is born stupid and is never going to figure out that no one is there to answer it, or else doesn't want to answer it. But a child who is suffering and has to let you know about it – that's another story.

Starting at birth

I was once assisting a very new crew who were helping a mother give birth to her first baby. I must add here it was also their first delivery after qualifying. Now, some babies have a small tissue-like covering on their heads called the operculum. This acts like Mother Nature's own crash helmet when the baby is in the birth canal. Often the operculum falls off as the baby progresses towards birth.

I was talking one of the crew members through the delivery and forgot to mention the operculum. The ambulance attendant was very nervous and visibly pale; his partner was standing behind us watching intently, looking equally unhappy. As the head crowned, the operculum dropped off – and so did the student who was standing behind the two of us! Needless to say, I assured the remaining crew member that it was okay, the head was intact, and it would advance any second now. Despite my assurances, he wasn't able to shed the familiar 'deer caught in the headlights' expression.

* * *

Births are always beautiful, but when a child dies, it is as if the future dies. This feeling was very poignant on one case I attended with my colleague Craig. Both he and his brother are excellent paramedics, almost legendary. Everyone had the greatest respect for them and you dared not mess up on a call. If Craig put his hand on your shoulder and said, "Cousin, why don't you go and sit in the car – I'll take over from here," you knew your career was just about over. In fact, your life was in the balance, depending on how bad it was, and you might have been better off just walking back to the station.

I was privileged to work with Craig before I applied to do my Critical Care Attendants course. He's not much of a conversationalist;

a man of few words with a quiet strength about him. On that occasion, we were sitting in the car listening to the radio. Then we heard a request for an ambulance to be dispatched to a place not far from where we were parked. The call was for a paediatric patient.

We soon heard the Ambulance radio back that the child had died. It had apparently been a choking. Without missing a beat Craig grabbed the mike and calmly asked "What is your 10-14 (location)?" The reply came through that they were in a doctor's rooms in the city. We rushed off, arriving in time to meet the ambulance crew just leaving, equipment in hand and looking very dejected.

Craig barged past them, demanding to know where the patient was. The doctor was writing out a death certificate. He was young and the expression on his face told it all. *This is not why I did medicine. I work in doctors' rooms so I don't have to do this kind of call.* He was visibly overcome with emotion.

We marched past him despite his protest that the child had died. We found the little girl on the examination table covered by a sheet. Craig pulled off the blanket, asking the history while he started to attach the ECG monitor.

"Where's the oxygen? What have you tried? How long have you been resussing this patient?"

The doctor had followed us in and told us that the child attended the nursery school crèche across the road. She was eating when she suddenly began to choke. When it was apparent that she couldn't breathe, one of the teachers scooped the child up in her arms and ran across the road to the doctors' rooms. Frantically, she deposited the now lifeless child in the frightened doctor's arms. The doctor examined her and decided there was nothing he could do.

Craig and I started working on the child despite the diagnosis. The ambulance crew came back in and looked at us strangely. It's not usual to go ahead and attempt resuscitation when a doctor has declared the patient dead.

And then we heard it – quite the most beautiful sound one can hear without a stethoscope. It was the sound of a heartbeat, picked up by the ECG machine. Sure enough, in a few minutes the unmistakable, rhythmical sound began to fill the room.

The ambulance crew were stunned. I couldn't stop shaking, and stopped compression on the chest. The doctor was another story. A vast number of emotions passed over his face in a matter of seconds. He went to his desk, put his head down and sobbed.

It is unfair to expect doctors to be pre-hospital specialists; their training is more geared to in-hospital medicine, unless they are trauma doctors. There is no doubt that South Africa has the most awesome training, and great medical schools. When I'm out of the country and meet up with a South African doctor, I'm never worried because I know they are more than qualified to deal with just about anything. But I did wonder how the guilt would affect him in the future, and I wondered if that little girl would realize that she had been given a rare second chance.

* * *

Kids at accident scenes can be demanding and at other times so innocently logical.

I arrived at an accident scene once to find the car a complete wreck; it looked a bit like one of those 3-D puzzles you assemble for the fun of it. After treating the occupants, who amazingly were not seriously hurt, I stood back like Leonardo da Vinci and surveyed this scrap-metal puzzle. I was wondering how one would explain this to the insurance company when I felt a tug on my arm and there was the youngest occupant of the car. About seven years old, he looked me straight in the eye and in his most earnest voice said, "Don't you worry, my dad works in a glue factory. He can glue it back together."

I have been called out to situations where children have been unbelievably brave in the face of the most extraordinary circumstances. I remember a motor vehicle accident where a mother, who was driving, was seriously injured. In the back was her little boy and a baby girl who was strapped into her car seat. Needless to say, the baby was very distressed and crying loudly. We extricated the little six-year-old boy out of the back window, and took him to the response car for treatment. We were wondering how to get the children to a family member who could take care of them. But he was having none of that – he walked back to the car with a badly injured knee. He stated firmly that he was not moving until we gave him his little baby sister so he could look after her. Once we had stabilized the two of them, he became concerned that there was no milk for the baby, who was now wailing. He asked if we could put some of the liquid from the intravenous bag that was in his mother's arm, in the baby's bottle!

* * *

As part of my job description when I was the liaison officer for the Johannesburg Ambulance Services from 1992–1993, I went to schools and taught children about the service. I told them what the telephone number for the ambulance service was, how to dial for an ambulance, and then showed them the inside of one. The thing they enjoyed most was standing on an intravenous drip bag, without it bursting, which afforded them much pleasure. I remember one child asking a very pertinent question: "How does the liquid come out the needle, when it's so small?"

I'll never forget the time I went to a school for hearing-impaired children and when it was time for me to let them hear the siren, I realised we had a problem and began to feel uncomfortable. But the teacher caught my eye and told all the kids to place their hands on the ambulance and 'feel the sound.' The delight on their faces reminded me how most of us take so many things for granted.

* * *

Children can get themselves into a difficult situation in the blink of an eye. I went on a call in the western suburbs one Sunday and found a little girl stuck in an old, unused top-loader washing machine. She was absolutely fine and concerned more about her Barbie who was wedged underneath her. Her parents, meanwhile, were running around frantically like headless chickens because they couldn't pull her out. After much pushing and pulling, scratching of heads, changing of plans and strategies – coupled with loud profanities on the part of the grandfather – we eventually decided to pour some lukewarm water with dishwashing liquid over her. This broke the surface tension of the water and worked very well, dislodging both the little girl and Barbie. And granddad – who was already nicely on his ear – was so happy that he needed no further excuse to down another brandy and coke, thank you very much.

* * *

Ellis Park is – or was in its heyday – a beautiful area, with gorgeous houses built in that wonderful South African style I love so much. They were kind of colonial, with wooden floors, lead windows, brass knobs, sash windows and those stoeps that wrap themselves halfway around the house. It's a very different picture nowadays.

We received a call from that area; the caller said a young child was in trouble, had stopped breathing. We flew there and were greeted by a beautiful German Shepherd, an unusual dog for the area. I also took in the well-kept lawn, nice car, and a little boy standing at the entrance, with a worried look on his face.

I was confronted by a frantic mother. Another child was lying on the floor, already turning a bluish colour and completely naked except for a pair of socks on her feet. I immediately attended to her air passage. Once that was sorted out she started to breathe shallowly and her colour began to come back.

While my crew were doing other things, I asked the mother how old the little girl was. She told me she was seven. When I looked at the child closely, she seemed very small for a seven-year-old. (I discovered later that the much larger boy was her twin brother.)

I questioned the mom further, asking if she had a medical condition because she was very thin and malnourished. I then began to see other things – and there was the distinct smell of rotten flesh. It became obvious that this child was not sick – she had been deliberately injured. There were cigarette burns on her skin, bruises over her ribs, and scars and scabs in different stages of healing all over her body. Her nails were torn and tufts of hair were missing from her scalp.

At this stage she was barely conscious and the mother became aware of my scrutiny, and started to interfere. She tried to switch my ECG monitor off, telling me I could now leave as she was breathing again. One of my crew took off her sock to do a blood glucose test and that's when we all saw the serious damage to her feet. They had been so badly burned that there were no soles left; there was a mass of pus and necrotic tissue adhering to the dirty sock. I felt a burning anger rise in me; I felt as if I'd just been kicked in the solar plexus.

I tried to maintain control as I noticed my crew also getting upset. This is the kind of moment when you can feel the wheels about to come off if you don't hold it together. Out of the corner of my eye I watched the crew slamming equipment and beginning to swear under their breath. By now, the mother was in my face again, and I could hardly bear to look at her as I told her we were taking the child to the nearest hospital. She started to argue and told me she had to stay at home because she was now breathing and she wouldn't allow her to be taken. I left a crew member to tell the mother she had better co-operate with us and let us take the child for treatment or the police would fetch her – and that we would take the child with or without her permission.

I walked back to my response car with a lump in my throat, fighting back tears. I felt as if I needed someone to open up my own air passage, because I couldn't breathe. My hands trembled and I felt a million emotions running through me too fast to categorize. Tears stung my eyes so badly that I couldn't see; I wanted to kick something, to feel some pain. But I couldn't find anything; instead I grabbed the pillow in my car and screamed my rage into it.

When the lump in my throat had subsided a little, my breathing eased, even though my head felt as if it was being hammered by a million little feet. I radioed ahead for the Child Protection Unit, and when we got to the hospital, they were waiting for us, with a camera and a docket waiting to be opened.

Later that day, I found out from the doctor treating this little patient, that this was not the first time she had been to that hospital. She had previously been removed from the care of her parents for a few months, and then returned. I visited her in the evening when I knocked off, taking her a colouring book and a soft toy. She told me she wanted to go home, that the nursing sisters had done these bad things to her.

I met some of her father's side of the family one night when I went to visit her again; they were all around the bed praying. I couldn't help but ask why they had let this heinous treatment of a little girl continue to this extent and how long were they going to wait before doing anything?[13] When would one of them have drawn the line between *I can't say anything* and *I must do something*? What made this case different to me was that they all knew about the abuse yet did nothing. They replied that I didn't know the father's temper. They would pray harder.

I walked away, shattered, feeling the weight of the world on me. There is a saying that I love: "You never stand as tall as when you stoop to help a child." That day I did not feel tall ...

I later found out that she had been sent to a home in the southern suburbs. I also read that her parents were so stoned reversing out of their driveway that they had had a fatal accident and never made it to court.

* * *

It is Sunday afternoon. I am in the response car talking nonsense with my very good friend Darren and two students. The conversation has now shifted from examining them to general chatter as we start to relax more.

Then at about two o'clock we receive that awful call – you get them every holiday without fail – a paediatric drowning.

As always, you arrive at a scene full of people milling around a limp little body. Sometimes someone is attempting to do CPR. The house was in a poorish suburb where the houses tend to be small with narrow driveways and tandem parking.

In this particular house they have a pool. I say pool, but I could just as well say pond as the water is so black that, were there more bodies

---

13 *Every Parent's Nightmare*, by Bruna Dessena, is a practical handbook on child abuse. It tells you what to do when abuse is suspected or disclosed. It is available in major bookstores and directly from the publisher on www.publisher.co.za.

under there, no one would be any the wiser. One can gather that there's a party on the go, either since that morning or remnants from the night before – there are bottles strewn on the patio, loud music is playing, and one person is passed out on a bench on the stoep.

I'm so grateful I'm with Darren. He is an instructor at the college and everything is very fresh in his mind as far as protocols and techniques are concerned. He tells me to do the airway as he does medication, and another ALS with us prepares the intravenous line, while the fourth crew member does chest compressions. She is a mom herself and I acknowledge how hard this must be for her; she has a child of the same age.

I am lying on the ground at the head of the child about to insert an endotracheal tube in her little throat, directly into her lungs. I can't help but notice how pretty she is, her hair done in beautiful braids. The ground beneath me is hard and biting into my elbows as I lean on them, ready to intubate her. So many things infringe on my consciousness – the smell of vomit compounded by heat, the wailing of the mother, the bleeping of the ECG monitor, the policeman raising his voice to the father, the suction machine next to me, the ambulance attendant trying to connect the oxygen tubing to the oxygen cylinder – I phase them out deliberately.

Preparing to intubate, I open her little mouth and find her throat is welling up with water and what looks like runny porridge. The suction machine can't keep up with all the fluid flooding the back of her throat.

When the larynx is touched by very cold water, it usually goes into a spasm to prevent any more water entering the lungs, but it can only do this for a few seconds. On this particular day the odds are against this little one; the water was too warm, her larynx didn't spasm and so water flooded her lungs and stomach simultaneously as she went under; this is known as a wet drowning. Sadly, it happened too fast for anyone to hear her, coupled with the fact that she obviously did not know how to swim.

Regardless, we continued fighting to get her back, trying for almost an hour. All of us, except Darren, are parents. The realization that it's not going to work this time hits you hard. You know you can never watch your kids every minute of the day. This case was a prime example of alcohol and lax attitude combining to create what would end in a predictable tragedy. I cannot emphasise enough as a paramedic, as a parent, as a concerned citizen – all kids must be strapped into cars, and all kids should be taught from an early age to swim. Teach them but don't impose your bad attitudes and fears on them.

* * *

One of the saddest calls involving a child I ever answered was in the southern suburbs. One late afternoon, just before the traffic started to get heavy, a mother had her four-year-old in the car, on the back seat, but not strapped in. She needed to post a letter and drove to the post box, which was on a nearby corner.

She side parked, got out of the car without locking it, and walked the short distance to the box. There were people all around, the area was busy and she didn't see her child climb out of the car to follow her.

She climbed back in and drove off. She was on a one-way street and needed to drive around the block to return facing in the right direction. In the meantime her child, probably becoming disorientated, crossed the road and was struck by a car travelling at high speed. The child was killed instantly.

By this time the mother had turned into the road and was now behind a few cars that had stopped for the accident. When she drew alongside the accident, she saw the child lying there and a passerby trying to revive him. She recognized the clothes; she stopped the car and climbed out. She ran towards the child screaming, inconsolable.

By the time I arrived on the scene the mother was clutching the child to her chest like a rag doll. She was covered in blood and no one could get near her. She was beyond consoling, beyond any form of reasoning. Can one reason with a human in their rawest, most painful moment? The answer is NO. This mother was trying to cope with guilt, grief, death, despair, anger at herself, anger at the driver, and anger at the child for leaving the car. Her heart had been ripped out of her chest for all to see, she was naked in her grief.

The bystanders weren't helping – they were simply watching the agonizing drama playing out in front of them. In a way they were feeding on the situation like sharks encircling wounded helpless prey. I approached her, she wouldn't make eye contact with me; and when she finally did she wouldn't maintain it long enough for me to open my mouth. She just got up and walked in and out of the traffic, not knowing what she was doing or where she was going. She just had to move – maybe the movement would bring her child back. She left a trail of blood behind her; she sat down, she stood up, she leaned against cars and just screamed.

It took everything in me not to cry; I could so understand her pain. The crowd was closing in; I had to try to get her to listen to me and move out of the road and onto the pavement. Out of the corner of my eye I saw the ambulance arrive.

I needed to get her to listen to me just for a few seconds so I could convince her to get into the ambulance, out of the public eye and out of danger. She was in a frenzy of grief; her emotions loud, raw and out of control. I was trying to be just the opposite. She knew there was nothing I could do to bring the child back; she wanted to be alone in her grief. She wanted life as she knew it to end, to die as quickly as her child had, and she wanted to be with her child, out of this ugly world.

She was filled with rage, and she transferred her anger to me. She began to swear at me and threaten me – if I came near her she would kill me. She would kill me if I took her child away; and interspersed with this she kept lifting the bloody face and kissing it. It was an incredibly heart-rending sight; it doesn't get rawer than this.

The presence of the police didn't help matters. I saw in her eyes the fear that they would take the child away by force if necessary. She had the look of a caged animal, an animal about to be darted.

In these traumatic events, there comes a moment when a shift happens, when the person suddenly surrenders to the inevitable, horrible truth; when they have to accept. She sat down on the road between two cars, all the raging energy of grief expended. I assessed her emotions and took the gap.

She remained sitting, oblivious to the stares, the hooting of cars, the people around her. She was the ground zero of this chaos around us.

I approached her cautiously, telling her in as steady a voice as I could muster, that I was not taking her child away. I sat down opposite her, saying nothing for a few agonizing minutes. I was acutely aware of many people staring at us, of the air filled with the smell of exhaust fumes and the familiar smell of fresh blood. I remember still the way the child's neck hung at a grotesque angle, the mother's face stained with blood and tears. My throat was aching, I found it difficult to breathe, this moment was too intimate – I wanted to run away. I wanted to be on an island in a hammock between two palm trees … instead I found myself in the back of the ambulance, doors shut, crying with her.

* * *

Nearing the end

Before one becomes accustomed to working in this great city of ours, before you acquire that street savvy that comes with years of working on and in the streets of Joburg, one is very naïve. You tend to think that every crime has a reasonable motive, every vagrant really is just poor and that drugs do not always play a part in the current situation. You are naïve enough to think that every comatose patient brought into the government hospital will be placed on a respirator or at least get an ICU bed.

I was still at this stage when I was dispatched to a call in Westcliff. I was the passenger that day, so I was preoccupied with doing that endless bane of my life – paperwork. My friend Johan was the driver. We arrived at a huge house with a Georgian-style exterior, stately and white, imposing against the grey sky. Lots of ivy choking the windows, a once well-kept lawn now grown so long that it bordered on neglect.

No-one came to the huge electric gates, and I began thinking this would make a great set for Edgar Allan Poe's "The Fall of the House of Usher." There was a beautiful old concrete birdbath shaped as two hands holding the water. Only there was no water in it. Here there were just remnants of an old English garden.

We finally got to the front door, which was slightly open. We waited patiently for someone to meet us. While we stood there, we became acutely aware of the most pungent smell – cat pee; very strong, almost intoxicating. It assaulted my nasal passages and we realized it was coming from inside. Johan looked at me, and gave me a nod. There was no one coming out to meet us, and after all, the door was slightly ajar.

We pushed the door open to be assailed by the worst smell I can ever remember. It hit us like a kick in the solar plexus. My eyes started to water because of the ammonia content. I was breathing through my mouth, thinking 'this is impossible – no one can possibly live here.'

The entrance hall had once been very grand; the tiles had turned from pristine white to dirty beige, but the inlay of black diamond-shaped tiles was still visible.

Three wild-looking cats of various ages skittered past us. The adjoining sitting room was dark; the drapes hadn't been opened in a long while, judging by the dust and grime collected in the folds. The worst was the dreadful squelching sound our boots made as we walked on the carpet. It was wet through, smelling as if buckets of vinegar had been splashed across it. It looked as if it had started out being attractive, had begun its life covered with some kind of paisley design, but that was long ago.

We continued to call out but were met with silence. There was a once-silver tray covered with a thick layer of dust – it now looked yellowish-brown. There were many framed photos of a family. The men had that old-fashioned middle parting in their sleek black hair and wore high collars. Soft, slightly effeminate hands holding walking sticks; and feet planted firmly apart in that patriarchal stance. Naturally there was also the standard photo of the good young woman sitting in a chair, with the protective husband behind her, hand close by to show they were married, but not too close to show any kind of impropriety. The frames were expensive, thick, dark, heavy wood.

It was then we heard a small sound, a faint moaning. We split up and searched the rooms. I found the kitchen and stood still to take it all in. An old, once-beautiful kitchen. The coal-burning stove was of yellowish enamel. The floor was covered in cat fur and cat excrement. There must have been at least twenty cat boxes with litter that hadn't been changed in ages.

A tap dripped inexorably; tea towels full of brown streaks hung dejectedly. There was a set of those lovely, old-fashioned fine-china tea cups, the ones with a gaudy fine gold design and burgundy border. The tea stains inside were dark and hard. The cake of soap in the sink had a layer of dust on it and those deep cracks that happen to soap when it is left to dry out.

The windows were opaque from the dirt. The cupboards were wooden, wall mounted, with fine mesh over the frame just hinting at what was inside. The knife on the table on the old dusty breadboard had an old-fashioned bone handle. Good old, well-made cutlery. The image that confronted us was distorted and difficult to hold in place because of the smell; the few cats that stayed behind in the kitchen were thin, nervous looking and very wary of me. My heart broke as I saw a litter of kittens under a hanging broom; they were lying on an old mealie meal sack. They were only a couple of days old. I was still breathing slowly; the smell overpowering, making it difficult to concentrate. The windows were closed, compounding the stench.

I heard Johan call out to me – he had found our patient. I joined him in a room further down the dark and smelly corridor. Two grey and black streaked cats leapt off a riempie stool halfway down the passage as I carefully made my way past. The fur left behind on the pillow was enough to make a wig. I entered the bedroom. I think the colour was oyster pink or salmon.

The room stood dark, a small bedside lamp illuminating the once grand interior. There was no TV. The bedside table was like a canvas of this old woman's life. No books, but lots of pills. An old clock, still ticking, a well-worn Bible, small and red. A jug of water, filthy on the outside, dust had settled on the miniscus. I looked over Johan's shoulder to see what he was doing.

There she was, so small she could have been mistaken for a child. She reminded me of a holocaust victim. Delicate, paper-thin skin with hands like fragile little birds, nails bent and yellow with thin, dark hairline fractures. Her hair thin, grey and oily around her dirty collar. That stale, old smell of paper and musty washcloths clung to her like a desperate shadow. The corners of her mouth were cracked, like the soap in the kitchen. She was dehydrated, her skin tenting on the surface of her hands. She had obviously lost a lot of weight, because her false teeth rattled around in her mouth as she tried to speak. Her pupils were pinpoints.

There were more cats on the bed, cat fur everywhere, long and of different colours; on the pillow, on her nightdress, on her blankets and her sheets. There were more litter boxes under the window and more cats in the walk-in closet. It looked like a cloud of soft hair as they moved in unison out of our way. Johan was trying to get a history from the poor woman, but we couldn't understand her. She was very weak and bordering on incoherent. We were trying to discover who had made the call for assistance, and where were they?

Suddenly, an old black woman walked into the room, giving us both a fright. She too was thin and old. She spoke to us in Afrikaans, telling us the madam must go to the hospital; she had had a fall last night. I then noticed the old lady's leg, a classic femur fracture – affected leg slightly inwardly rotated, shorter than the unaffected one. The patient didn't even complain of pain as we transferred her to the stretcher.

The domestic worker didn't seem to notice the cats; she already had the patient's overnight bag ready for the hospital. She seemed to want the patient out of the house as quickly as possible. The old lady, on the other hand, couldn't make decisions for herself, couldn't speak for herself, and couldn't even tell us that she wanted to be left there with her beloved cats, which is what I felt she would have said if she could. However, we couldn't leave her with a fractured leg.

She asked nothing, ate like a bird, and made no noise. She had been forgotten by her family. Her drugs were probably fed to her before the previous dose had worn off so there was no escape for her. No escape from outside people who made decisions for her, decided what was good for her, didn't worry too much about whether she was happy or not – as long as she was manageable. She would probably die in hospital alone, without much ceremony. I wondered if she could hear people talking about her in her drugged stupor; was it like walking under water, trying to see through the blur, trying to make out the muted sounds?

Before that call, I was naïve enough to assume that all old people are taken care of by their family; that no one would leave their loved ones to deteriorate like that.

* * *

This incident was a mixture of funny and strange, depending on which side you were on. I was once called out to Jabavu Station in Soweto. Now, working in Soweto is a whole new ballgame. Here the addresses are given as 3241 Piri, with no street names. There are, thankfully, no high-rise buildings, so no carrying of patients up and down stairs. The community spirit is beautiful – *Ubuntu*[14] in action.

I receive the call as a gunshot wound. It is the early hours of the morning so this can only mean that a burglar has been nailed or it's a lovers' quarrel. Why do they always fight in the early hours? It seems to me these hours are reserved for quarrels, asthma attacks and croup.

I'm on my way to the petrol station in Jabavu; it's not a great distance from where I was. I arrive and find no one, not even the petrol attendants to greet me in their usual semi-sleepwalking state. It looks like a situation that just screams, "Please rob me." I stay in my car and wait a few minutes, taking in my surroundings. Normally, if there's been a shooting, the area would be crawling with cops. Unless, of course, the

---

14 Desmond Tutu described *Ubuntu* as "... the essence of being human. *Ubuntu* speaks particularly about the fact that you can't exist as a human being in isolation. It speaks about our interconnectedness. You can't be human all by yourself, and when you have this quality - *Ubuntu* - you are known for your generosity."

spurned lover who did the dirty deed has waited for the last gasp before calling the ambulance. Strangely, there is no one about, and it's also quiet – not even that gentle sound of Radio FM in the background. I get out of my response car, hands in pockets, and walk towards the office. On the way I notice a stationary car parked at the very far end near a petrol pump that is normally reserved for huge trucks.

I walk to the office, peer inside and come face to face with the petrol attendants, all gagged, tied up and with eyes like saucers. Because I think I'm the last missing Charlie's Angel, my first thought is to get the poor blighters out of their unfortunate situation and find out what happened. While freeing everyone, I realize that the logical action would have been to fly out of there because the person or persons responsible might still be hanging around, ready to tie me up next.

After the thank-yous have been said and the cops radioed to come out – and almost having a monument built for me – I walk back to my car glad to feel that I'd been useful. It is then that I realize that the car I'd seen earlier is still parked there. Something tells me in that weird way it does (I'm a woman, after all) to walk to the car and see what the story is. Now you would have thought I might have been cautious enough not to go investigating cars parked at odd angles. But no – the pull of the curious and the strange is such a force within all Scorpios that I simply cannot leave it alone. We are attracted to the risky, the unspoken, the weird in this great Noah's Ark of humanity that inhabits our little planet.

It doesn't take me long to see that the two men in the front seat are very dead. The cause – gunshots to the chest and head. Behind them is a frail, little old man. Yes, he might have been old and frail, and yes, he did drive a *skorokoro*[15], but what spirit!

---

15 Worn and ragged beyond its years, usually used to describe a vehicle

The amazing story that unravelled was that the two thugs held up the petrol station attendants – on foot – and when said old man came to fill up his car on his way to his homeland, he was confronted by these two thugs, whom profilers would describe as 'seriously unprepared and disorganized'. They had come to rob a petrol station with no advance plan about their getaway. They had grabbed him, shoved him in the back seat and proceeded to argue about where they were going to spend the money first. So intense was their argument that they didn't notice the *gogo*[16] pull out a .38 Special and plug them both. Three cheers for all those who work night shift and get to meet real heroes!

* * *

If you have a love for the city of Johannesburg and its beautiful old buildings as I do, you never tire of looking at them. Every time I get a call in the city I still marvel at the once-elegant buildings, their sturdy columns and thick concrete designs. I am particularly fond of those small black and white tiles that adorn some of the entrances; the brass door knobs; those light switches that make a very loud click when you flick them; the intricate lead glass designs in some of the old churches; the beautiful wooden doors and lintels, and the equally divine parquet flooring.

I was happy to be called out as back-up one day to one such lovely old building. It was a block of flats and the entrance was adorned by a very intricate mosaic done in black and white; its lifts were the old-fashioned kind with an outer sliding metal gate, then the glass doors. Had they not requested me specifically for this call, I would have missed the opportunity to see such fine craftsmanship. It was an all-

---

16   Old man

male crew who had asked for me, which made me suspect it was a rape or a child who had been abused. It is a given that my colleagues call me to deal with such things as I have the connections and know the system backwards.

As I got out of the lift my nostrils were assaulted by a strong smell of what I thought was vinegar. My first thought was that it must be some kind of gas leak. But why was everyone still inside the flat where the smell was so powerful? Had everyone forgotten what they were taught?

I came face to face with a number of firemen as they walked out of the flat and observed their expressions. This becomes an automatic thing – it's always a good indicator of the nature of what has happened. If they are guffawing and making loud jokes about ordering out, then I know it must be a particularly bloody scene; if they are all sucking in their stomachs then there must be a gorgeous woman in distress. An hysterical female would have them come out wringing hands, and if they're mincing and flopping their wrists they are mocking some obviously gay guy. I know that it's usually a child when they come out sombre and don't meet my gaze.

But the looks that met me that night were different; a mixture of silence and disbelief. I headed towards the room where most of the crew were busy. I noticed a little old man, quietly dignified, belonging to that wonderful old-fashioned group who thought a bow tie the height of sartorial elegance. He was sitting on a sofa in the lounge and I heard him ask: "Will she be all right? She and I have been friends for many years; we have no family, you know – just each other." He seemed to be speaking to everyone and no one.

I reached the bathroom and took a look at my patient. She was an old lady, slumped forward holding herself up by her elbows at the tap end of the bath. She was extremely pale and weak, and I noticed blood between her legs. A fireman handed her a blanket, which she didn't even take, a very telling negative factor. It told me that her level of consciousness was so low that she wasn't really aware of being naked in front of all these firemen.

I got the details of what happened from the senior fireman. He told me she went to have a bath at around four in the afternoon. She was getting out of the bath when she suddenly felt very weak and in one movement turned and sat down. She misjudged the space and managed to sit on the taps. I asked him why no one had removed her yet and was told they couldn't. This poor woman had impaled herself on the tap. Nothing could be done until the water supply to the building had been turned off. And they were also waiting for the jaws of life to cut the tap away from the wall. I waited for my cerebrum and cortex to connect this information.

Because there was a delay, I decided to investigate myself, not waiting for any more neurons to fire. The bath was on my left with the basin next to it. I squatted down and lifted her left buttock to see what had happened. The tap head and straight piece had penetrated the perineal lining[17]. The tap was so deeply embedded that only the spout was visible. Anxiously looking at my watch, I realized that she had been impaled for close on five hours, a dangerously long time. This was the reason for the vinegar odour caused by her high sugar levels. When I tested it, her sugar level was 19mm/mols – a normal reading is between 4 and 7.

The only reason she was found at all was because of the little old man sitting on the sofa outside. He came to watch the soaps with her every day, and realized something was amiss and alerted the police. After the arrival of the jaws of life and much strategizing, we cut the tap from the wall and took her to hospital like that.

---

17   The area between the anus and the vagina

There wasn't a happy ending, however. Very sadly, she passed away three days later from internal bleeding.

* * *

I remember another call, also involving old people in an old building.

There are so many things people get touchy about, and so often when a person dies, we have such regrets about the really stupid things we all argue about. So many people find themselves saying "Oh, I wish I'd never said that to him ..."

So there I was, on my way to the block of flats in Hillbrow to investigate 'suspicious circumstances'. I was met by a little old lady, probably in her eighties. She told me that she had shared the flat with her brother for many years, and that they had had a big argument a couple of days previously. A fleeting thought went through my mind – what on earth do siblings argue about at eighty plus?

She asked me to sit down, and feebly told me that the argument had happened about two to three days before. She was still most annoyed that he had not spoken to her; in fact she had not seen him for three days. She had even been gracious enough to make him food and place it on a tray outside his bedroom door. And he did not eat it! This just naturally added fuel to the fire.

My sensitive nostrils had already detected an odour emanating from his room. The door was closed and I could tell that her brother was never going to eat another meal. I looked around and took in the flat – loads of family photos, beautiful parquet flooring, tasselled rugs strategically placed under heavy, ornate ball-and-claw wooden furniture. In a corner there was a small TV with two chairs, and two aluminium trays on collapsible tables next to each chair. These things told the whole story. Without knowing them, one could see that every night they would watch TV together and have their meal. As brother

93

and sister, obviously with no living parents, staying in the city, they were virtual prisoners; like so many of the old folk whose families had emigrated and moved on.

Without examining her, I realised that she had lost her sense of smell. She would otherwise have placed a call to the undertakers. I wasn't sure what to do first – break it to her gently that he had already died, or go in and come out and tell her. I decided on the latter.

He had locked himself in his room so we needed to use a crowbar to open the door. There he was, a dignified old man, wearing socks and shoes even though he was just at home; a nice pressed shirt and his hair tidily combed back. He was surrounded by what he loved – old clocks and old clock radios. Lots of them. He sat in his chair, alongside an old makeshift workbench. His head drooped onto his chest; in one hand he held a screwdriver. He died doing what he most loved doing, peacefully. No sign of struggle, no trying to get to the door.

This call left a huge impression on me. And since then I have arrived so many times in answer to a call and heard the family say, as they talk around the body, "I never had time to say goodbye," "I regret having gone to bed angry with her," "If I'd only known how short a time we had left."

* * *

7

The trauma of trauma work

THERE are so many times in the course of my job that I am exposed to the rawest of human emotions. So often I am there at the precise moment when the emotional wheels come off. There are agonizing minutes between the event and the realization by the family member that their loved one has really gone.

Coping mechanisms

I've seen it so many times that I know the process well. I watch them lose control, and fold; then comes resignation and a kind of acceptance. This is purely temporary – later they will go through all the stages of grief: denial, anger, bargaining, depression and finally acceptance. But for now they realize that that person will not be in their future, the hours and days to come will not contain them.

Witnessing it so often doesn't make it any easier; I still feel the tightening in my throat every time. My knuckles still go white as I squeeze my stethoscope – always a comfort and a distraction.

I suppose in every profession there are people who become immune to what they do; they lose the passion and just come to work to receive a salary. When I first started in the Ambulance division, it was the duty of the paramedics to take the patient to the morgue. The intelligentsia in our legal system at the time also made an addendum to that law that even if a patient was in a million pieces the medic had to pick up the pieces and bring the offensive pile to the doctor to have it declared dead. Naturally we sought out the youngest, most inexperienced doctors to do this difficult task, and, just as one would expect, every time they came up with the most ingenious and inventive excuses.

One Sunday we were called to a gunshot head; and as usual, on arrival, there was not much left of the head. It was a grotesque injury. All gunshot heads are unforgettable images, all are grotesque and macabre, and I always feel huge empathy with the family members who have to identify the victim.

Very often there are photographs somewhere of the deceased person, giving an indication of what they had looked like before this tragedy. I always find this juxtaposition quite eerie.

So there I was at this particular incident, retrieving all the pieces to be certified, while my colleague – who was one of those people who had lost his passion and any sensitivity he might ever have had – ambled over to the pile I had amassed and poked at it without gloves. The unfeeling so-and-so then proceeded to order me to look for the other eye. I eventually found part of it staring straight back at me from under the edge of the curtains, like something out of a Roald Dahl story. Yes, that's right – you've got to love this job.

I was brought up short by a friend recently, who picked me out for using the term 'gunshot head'.

"It's not a gunshot head – it's a person with a serious injury – maybe a fatal one," she said.

I had to think about it for a while because to me it's a term we use in the field to identify an injury. One definitely becomes inured to the fact that one is dealing with a person, a member of a family – son, husband, maybe even a daughter. I don't think we would be able to cope if we saw each 'gunshot head' in personal terms. In this country, which has the highest murder rate in the world, one has to build up some sort of defence system, or you'd break down yourself. As it is, many paramedics suffer from depression themselves because of the ongoing trauma they're exposed to.

If you consider that an average of 56 murders occur every day in South Africa, that's a lot of carnage. And incidentally, that figure has reduced considerably. At one stage it was nearer to 70 per day.

The desperate and deliberate

In this privileged profession, we are very often the first people on the scene after a tragedy has occurred, so it is not unusual to witness the sad and depressing side of human behaviour. When one sees people die in accidents – people who wanted to live, people with families who need them, but are taken anyway – well, it's difficult then to process that there are also people who just can't face another day, regardless of the family they leave behind. There are souls who are so tormented that they are driven to extreme acts. Every suicide note I've ever read echoes my own sentiments on some days. At times these acts are impulsive and at others they are very well thought out.

One of the strangest suicides I ever heard of was one that happened at the Ponte building in Hillbrow. The building, being so high, became a favourite spot – if one can put it like that – for people who wanted to be sure of ending their lives. This one wasn't my call; my colleagues told me about it. They were confronted by a truly bizarre sight – a man had jumped and had managed to land on his feet, which was extremely unusual. The impact was so great that his femurs (thigh bones) went up through his rib cage and were sticking out straight up, like two antennae on either side of his neck.

I also remember the determination of one man living in a rather affluent area. Presumably, he had thought it through properly, because he had planned his own demise down to the last detail. He had decided to use gas, so at least it was a 'clean death'. He planned to do it on the domestic worker's day off, and waited for all the members of his household to leave for school and work. He took a section of pipe from the Creepy Krauly, then fashioned a perfect-sized hole for the pipe in a piece of cardboard. He then rolled down the back window of his car enough to accommodate the cardboard and pipe. Then he proceeded to weld the garage door shut from the inside.

He had written letters to everyone; he had a photo album on the passenger seat next to him. He swallowed a handful of valiums with whiskey, turned on the ignition of the car and waited for the end to come.

He needn't have died; if he'd changed his mind and decided to live, he could have – because someone who loved him tried to raise the alarm. His trusty Jack Russell, faithful friend, was outside the garage barking incessantly. We were called, but when we tried to get in, we found he'd welded the window and door very thoroughly and there was no access.

Sometimes deliberate acts have very unexpected results. Once, on a night shift with students in the car, just slowly cruising Hillbrow, I stopped at a robot and a man ran towards us, shouting and pointing at something across the road. We stopped and got out. He told us there was a man who was going to jump. We were all looking upwards at the building; visibility was bad as it was a rainy night.

I then realized that the man had already jumped; he was caught on the palisade fence. As he had landed he had folded over four of the spikes. I rushed over, and amazingly, he was conscious and spoke to me. What was even more amazing was that he was able to prevent himself from sliding further down. Very bizarre to see, and very difficult to erase from one's memory. He was removed from the spikes but later died in theatre – he had just lost too much blood.

* * *

The statistics for suicides in South Africa are horrendous. According to a book by Professor Lourens Schlebusch called *Suicidal Behaviour in South Africa*, published in 2005[18], there are between 6 800 and 8 000 suicides in our country annually. Broken down, this translates into 667 deaths per month, or 22 every single day! Almost one every hour, around the clock ...

Internationally, amongst the statistics of femicide – women who are killed by their intimate partners – between 20% and 40% of the perpetrators will commit suicide afterwards. There don't seem to be comparable statistics for South Africa, but we read about it often enough in the media to know that our statistics don't look much different.

And equally horrifying are the stats for unsuccessful suicide attempts. Every month there are more than 13 000 people who try to kill themselves, but fail. This comes down to 438 per day, or 18 every

---

18 Five or more years later, the figures have probably remained proportionately high, if not higher.

hour![19] This is mind-boggling. Perhaps we should all be more mindful of the people around us, especially at vulnerable times like Christmas, which is notorious for its increased death toll. People kill themselves for complex reasons that are sometimes difficult to fathom. And sometimes the reasons are simple. For instance, a young person might commit suicide for fear of not passing exams, and an old person do so because they're desperately lonely.

Speaking of desperation, how about the man who booked into a casino, gambled away all of his money, then went to his room and shot himself?

* * *

Taking the family with you

Thankfully, one of the traumas that I haven't had to deal with often is family murders. These are very horrendous events, and South Africa seems to have more than its fair share. For some reason, it seems to affect the Afrikaans population more, although in the last year or two, there have been many more incidents involving Black policemen – perhaps because so many more have joined the police force, they handle weapons all the time, and it seems like a solution. There are statistics that prove that most of the perpetrators who kill their intimate partners are not white-collar workers, but more likely to be in the police or security industry.

---

19   If you, or anyone you know, needs help, call the Depression and Anxiety Group on 0800 567 567.

There are far more femicide cases than there are full-scale family murders. But South Africa once again has the dubious honour of being way ahead of any other country in this field.

However, I was surprised to discover that in Italy, a criminologist, Professor Francesco Bruno, did research that showed that family murders went up by between 10% and 20% in very hot weather. He said that dehydration is a driving factor, because the brain can't regulate violent impulses so easily. People suffering from depression or schizophrenia are more at risk when the temperature soars.

Seeing that we have such high temperatures in South Africa during our summer months, I wonder if that has anything to do with it?

I remember a few years ago that there were three family murders in one week! Is it because human life has so little value, or is it because guns are so easily available? Or could it be the fact that violence is so prevalent now that it's become more 'acceptable'. A shocking truth is that 50% of all women murdered are done away with by their husband or intimate life-partner.

How a parent can shoot or smother their own child is unfathomable to me. If your own life is unbearable, it's your choice to end it – but why take away the chance that the rest of the family might have at a better life?

When I've had to deal with such a situation, I've found it very difficult to make the pictures in my mind go away. I seem to remember every little detail. Every bloody scene is permanently imprinted on your retinas until you close your own eyes forever.

Overriding everything, there are always smells and colours that permeate your consciousness – the acrid smell of gunpowder, and the colour and smell of blood everywhere. A thick patina of both settles over the whole tragic canvas. There will be scores of police and forensic experts crawling around the scene like ants. And somewhere in the house, you'll come across photographs on a side table or a mantelpiece showing happy, smiling faces. It adds the most macabre touch to an already unreal situation.

The worst is finding children lying face down in their beds, sometimes still holding a well-worn soft toy that is now covered in blood. Other toys stare at you from the shelves, also splattered with dark blood – silent witnesses to the before, during and after events.

You walk into a child's bedroom and find little cars strewn on the floor as carelessly as the body that is lying in the passage face down, showing the direction in which he tried to run away. Fluorescent lights leave no shadows on the blood running down the walls, making the goriness completely unreal.

* * *

I had a friend who worked in the police force and we would sometimes meet up while we were both on standby and have coffee at one of the garages dotted around the beautiful city of Johannesburg. One night we were enjoying hot dogs when he received a call about shots having gone off somewhere not far away. He invited me to come with him, and since I wasn't doing anything, I followed him in my response car.

When we arrived at the house, situated in a cul-de-sac, the dog unit was on the scene. I could see from the body language and faces of the cops that this was not pretty. The first thing a cop said to me was: "There are five inside."

I opened my boot to remove my bag and he looked at me and said: "Five dead."

I followed him in and walked past the body of an older woman lying in the lounge, cellphone clutched in dead fist. The next room contained a small boy holding a soft toy, gunshot to the side of his head. Next tragedy – a young girl with gunshot to the back of her head; she was facing away from the wall, and had long hair, now matted with blood. The last one was an older boy with David Beckham posters on the wall and a hockey stick near the door – gunshots to the head and chest.

And then, inexplicably, we found the father, perpetrator of this horror, in his bedroom. He had shot the family, and then put the gun to his own head. The smell of cordite was heavy in the air, the tragedy of it all weighing all around us like a heavy burden. While I was standing there trying to process this incomprehensible scene, I heard a loud exclamation from down the passage. "What the eff is this?"

I edged closer and noticed a policeman from the canine unit with a dog, straining at the leash, his body tense. I went right up to them. I looked into a room that was not a normal room with a floor; the whole area was a swimming pool between the four walls, with a very narrow edging from the door that opened from the passage we were standing in. It was tiled black, the edge so close to the wall that if you didn't know there was a pool, you would have fallen in.

It wasn't deep and the lights in this supposed room were not bright. Shining our torches over the water revealed a pentagram painted on the bottom of the pool. In the corners was another design I could not make out. I didn't wait to see the rest, but left quickly. It's one thing to see dead bodies, it's entirely different to see unexplained evil. I tried to reason it away by telling myself that maybe they had been shooting a film or something. But it's useless – you know when there's something very wrong. Even the reaction of the dog told me that. That call kept me awake for many a night after that; but even more disturbing was the fact that no mention of that event was ever reported in any newspaper.

* * *

As a paramedic I have done my fair share of movie standbys, working at parades, rugby matches, and special events. I've even done shifts at

Gold Reef City and Montecasino. It is a given that in this job you will see human beings in their rawest moments and most desperate states. It is a given you will encounter people who live by the philosophy, "It won't happen to me."

Casinos are mind-blowingly beautiful, albeit artificial, in their design. Every artifice is used to part you from your hard-earned money. There are bright lights to disorientate people so they don't realize how late it actually is. Drinks are brought to you; all you have to do is pump your family's much-needed financial nest egg into this hungry machine. Here people gamble into the wee hours of the morning; they sit on the little chair in front of that machine for hours; some will not even go to the toilet in case someone else takes that 'lucky' slot.

Many a time people will fake chest pains after they have gambled away all they own; then in the ambulance on the way to hospital they ask the driver to drop them at home because they are feeling better.

Some people have no shame, gambling into the small hours while their children are lying on a bench outside the gambling pit. It happens on school nights too; both parents are gambling and no one is watching the children. The kiddy care centre closed long ago and there are children still in school uniform, giving indication of how long they've been there, often hungry, just waiting for their parents.

At Montecasino I had a boss who felt no compunction about smashing the windscreen of a parked car to gain access to a child inside. There are parents who feed cough syrup to their children so that the children will sleep, leaving them free to gamble. They think no one will know the child is there – the windows are tinted, and the car is parked far away from the entrance. They don't count on the child waking up a lot earlier when the cough syrup has worn off. The security guards alert us; they've been trained to listen out for crying children, and keep an eye on cars with tinted windows parked in the distance.

* * *

War stories

It's very enlightening as well as entertaining to sit in a group of experienced paramedics and hear what they fear. We all unanimously agree we don't ever want to treat someone we know. This is a given.

We all agree drunken patients are the most obnoxious. We concur that we are not in this job for the money but to gather brownie points to go to heaven as we spend our free time erring on the side of hedonistic sins, too much smoking and disregarding family time as we are always at work ...

We all agree that vomit and feeling around in the contents doesn't freak us out; we are happy (well, I don't mean smiley-happy) to put our fingers in warm bullet holes, hold a severed body part, or insert an intravenous needle in the dark – but there are just some things we cannot do.

I, for one, cannot clip dogs' nails. I also cannot watch a wildlife documentary showing a kill, but am happy to watch a gruesome Quentin Tarantino film. I cannot watch Idols or any programme where humans are degraded, even if they choose to be there. I once caught a glimpse of Cheaters – a reality show. Well, it took me a long time to recover from that one.

I suppose many jobs have their occupational hazards, but being a paramedic has to be rather high on the list. You can spot an old medic far away – they are the ones with back problems. It comes from years of working in places like Hillbrow, where people live in buildings with lifts that no longer work and where, coupled with Murphy's Law, the patient will be the heaviest and live on the top floor. It's no mean feat carrying a patient in a sitting position down thirteen flights of stairs. Try lifting a stretcher higher than waist level into an ambulance that is parked on an incline.

Back problems are a true sign of having served time in such places, but there are many other indications. We compare war wounds like trophies. I have a scar on my right knee from a piece of windscreen that went right through my pants and embedded itself under my knee cap. This happened at an accident scene while trying to put a collar on a patient in an area with almost no lighting.

We also bear scars of patients' assaults; I have three on my face. It takes a special kind of miscreant to call for an ambulance and then attack you because she says you've stolen her apples. Or there are the even more endearing people who set their dogs on you because they don't want to go to hospital. And if you sometimes wonder why they don't make the uniforms more feminine, well it's a war zone we're working in.

And we've all heard about the medics who have continued to treat patients in the midst of gang cross-fire, or those who have been killed (or nearly killed) by oncoming motorists whilst attending to victims at the scene of an accident, or even, as has happened more recently, raped whilst on duty, attending to a patient!!!

I have also had to attend many calls that have had sexual overtones, or perhaps I should say undertones. I love the drunk ones who want to marry me, and insist on holding my hand; or, even better, those who exude smelly, alcoholic fumes, but who seriously try to kiss me.

* * *

As medics we sometimes forget how traumatic a cut or severed finger can be to a child or someone not used to blood. Because we are so used to seeing that as non life-threatening, we fail to respond as we should.

I remember a call in Riverlee at the train station. A commuter had been standing in the train about to climb off, when the rail he was

106

holding on to somehow got entangled with his ring and the keys he was holding. He managed to amputate his ring finger.

I arrived, packaged his finger, put him in the ambulance and proceeded to the nearest trauma unit. Being the ever resourceful Girl Guide I am, I remembered that there was a hotel bottle store on the way, so there would be some ice available.

As we approached the bottle store I grabbed the packaged finger and ran inside to ask for some ice. The manager asked how much ice I was looking for. While I was trying to tell him that I only needed a few cubes, just enough to place this finger in till I could get it to the hospital, he passed clean out in front of me.

Silly man, he didn't seem to know it's rude to go from the vertical to the horizontal while someone's talking to you. Very inconsiderate – I now had two patients. And then, to make matters worse, some of the employees came walking onto the scene, very worried looks on their faces, to see what I'd done to their boss. Why was he prostrate on the floor? I was so tempted to show the finger and watch the Mexican wave happen in front of me. But I resisted as I knew it was crucial to get the patient reunited with his finger as soon as possible.

* * *

The serious side of this job takes all one's courage and energy, and there are certainly some nerve-wracking times. There are times spent staring intently at an ECG monitor, and even more moments listening intently, having to use all one's senses, observing the slightest changes, nuances, sounds and smells.

So we make the most of the more light-hearted scenarios, as when a child has shoved a peanut far up her nose and is laughing while her mother is hyperventilating and screaming: "I will smack you into the middle of next week (a la Cosby's mother), I've told you not to eat and run at the same time ...".

* * *

8

Working in a greater team

IN emergency work, you are acutely aware that the quality of treatment depends not only on the paramedics but on everyone involved in the incident. This can include the police, the traffic department, pilots, specialist rescue teams, doctors and nurses.

Up in the air

As in any country privileged enough to have an emergency helicopter service, the crew who work on these services are a very dedicated bunch, giving up their Sundays, holidays and nights to do shifts on the helicopter for the sheer love of it. It takes enormous courage and nerves of steel for the pilot to put down the helicopter in the tightest of spots, or to land at night when one cannot see overhead power lines. He is completely dependent on the instructions of the senior paramedic bringing him in, as they normally know the area very well. I wonder how many ordinary citizens appreciate how fortunate we are to have such facilities?

The same goes for the mountain and water rescue teams and the diving units. These consist of volunteers who are on constant standby. When the call comes in it's usually quite serious: someone trapped in the mountains, or fallen off a ledge, or gone overboard into the water. Or, a dicey one – a microlight gone down a ravine.

These people then leave their jobs, warm beds, movies or family functions, get into their gear, and make the journey to a central point. They race against time knowing that every minute counts as hypothermia can set in very quickly, or the patient might be haemorrhaging.

The mountain rescue teams spend days at a time searching for missing people and more often than not, they are called upon to perform stressful tasks, packaging and removing patients or dead bodies when they're found. Inevitably, this is never on a flat surface within easy reach or where a helicopter can land easily. They carry these strangers for many kilometres, over tough terrain, in rain and cold, and all for the love of it.

I truly admire and have the utmost respect for them. I have noticed there is a particular kind of person who is drawn to a calling where you wear a uniform, love discipline, work well as a team and outperform yourself under stressful conditions. These brave men and women are truly dedicated and give unconditionally.

* * *

When I was a volunteer on the emergency helicopter I always remember those clear summer evenings as we took off and were able to fly with the windows open, and see the wonderful lights of the city below. We would circle above the glittering lights of Hillbrow, over the Randburg Waterfront and then follow the M1 North towards Pretoria.

One of the pilots who flew our emergency helicopter was an ex-police pilot, a wonderful man. He was as tough as nails and wore size 17 shoes (as the saying goes) but he had a small idiosyncrasy, one that he was embarrassed about, but couldn't control. He was squeamish.

One day he flew a group of us to fetch a patient who had been trapped in a car for more than 20 minutes following an accident. The patient's foot had been severed.

After the patient had been treated and prepared for flight, we all climbed aboard. The sister had been guarding the tail rotor, so she was the last to climb in. She got in, with the patient's severed foot in a bag, which she deposited at her feet, just centimetres away from the pilot. As with all flying, the most critical times are taking off and landing, and the heli crew adheres to a strict code of conduct, maintaining absolute silence.

The pilot had done all his communications and was lifting off when he casually asked the sister what was in the bag. She was doing the paperwork and absent-mindedly told him. A loud and very ungraceful thud followed when the pilot passed out and the heli hit the ground. We were left with painful butts, laughing and swearing at the sister for forgetting his little problem. We waited for the pilot to come around and in a few minutes we were on our way again, all very quiet and feeling a bit like naughty kids.

* * *

One night we were called urgently to a small town outside Johannesburg where we were to fetch an accident victim and transport her to the nearest trauma centre for treatment. After about twenty minutes flying time in the helicopter we landed and made our way to the local casualty, where we were confronted by half the population of the small town. The patient was a little girl of about five or six who had been in the car with her pregnant mom when their car hit a pedestrian. The child had not been strapped in and she went through the windscreen, coming to land a good few metres away from the car. Because her face was very distorted from the impact it was proving difficult for the doctor to gain an airway and secure it.

As in all small towns the people are very hospitable and this was no different. While we struggled to get her stable, tea was made and brought right into the resus room! Once we stabilized her and loaded her into the helicopter, we took off. Her parents went ahead in their car – they had family near the trauma centre, with whom they could stay. Unfortunately, however, they did not have a cellphone.

On the way there, the patient started to deteriorate very quickly. After a gallant effort on everybody's part, we lost her.

The law states that you cannot drive a dead body through, or fly it over, a city – you have to have the nearest hospital declare that the person is deceased. Now this was a little ridiculous as we had a doctor with us. Nevertheless, we decided to land in the nearest town. There was no landing light, and overhead power lines are nigh invisible at night. The pilot managed to land the helicopter in the well-lit parking lot of a shopping centre.

Then our troubles began as the hospital refused responsibility for the body because the death did not take place there. Everyone was becoming tense as we realized that the family were on their way to the trauma centre and we wouldn't be able to fly there. The head of the flight service had contacted us, very belatedly, to say we had to fly her to a hospital in Johannesburg, not the one the parents were going to. Everyone, including the pilot, had a good cry before we got back into the heli. Our hearts went out to the parents who would now have to be sent back to Joburg. And then there was the utter frustration of not being able to contact them and let them know what had happened!

* * *

Having a cellphone can save valuable time. One morning, my good friend and paramedic colleague Mark and I were on our way home. We had both had a really busy night shift; stocks had run out and we were so exhausted we decided to leave our bags at the station, preferring to come in early for the next shift that night. We had a lift club so there we were on our way home in his car, with nothing in the way of equipment on us, not even a pair of gloves. As we crossed a busy intersection we came across a huge accident.

Cursing loudly at our lack of equipment, I went over to the woman lying on the road and Mark went off to the other car, reporting back that there was a child with a serious head injury. I got on my cellphone and called the helicopter directly; I was lucky to reach the pilot as he was doing his preflight checks and within a few minutes they were at our scene. The tow-truck guys helped cordon off the landing zone, and a week later the child was discharged from hospital. Sometimes it is permissible to pull rank and use your buddies.

* * *

While still on the subject of cellphones, I was once on my way to one of my favourite fly-fishing resorts for the Easter weekend. My friend and colleague, Glenda, a very competent paramedic, was travelling in her own car behind me as she was going to be joining me. We stopped along the way for coffee, and then, shortly after resuming our journey, we came across an accident.

It must have just happened, as the wheels of the upturned car were still turning when we both jumped out to investigate. The driver had successfully managed to find the only stretch of water alongside the highway. In fact, he must have been admiring it, and not looking where he was going. He had gone down the embankment, over a barbed wire fence, and right into it. He was lying face down in the muddy reeds, having sustained a severe head injury. He was not wearing a seatbelt and one can just imagine the violent forces that had acted on his body before the car finally stopped rolling.

Glenda and I ran down the embankment. She was clothed from head to toe in a beautiful white linen suit, not expecting to be on duty. I was struggling through the wire fence hampered by my bag. I also forgot that I had my gun strapped to my ankle. We reached the unfortunate man and managed to turn him over. In addition to his serious injuries, he had aspirated a lot of the muddy water. His lungs were really not sounding too healthy ... they sounded like a coffee percolator.

I got on my phone and managed to contact the helicopter directly. Within minutes they were on their way. Glenda and I struggled to get him up onto the highway, then cordoned off the traffic. We worked on him, but things weren't going well. We went on trying for another twenty minutes until the helicopter arrived. The doctor we had requested declared the man dead very soon after he saw him. As we began packing up, I realized that my cellphone was missing, and my new shoes and gun were both soaking wet.

And then a strange thing happened. The hooter of the car that had crashed started blaring – and there was absolutely no-one near it! It felt as if the man was trying to say something – maybe thank you for trying. I don't know, but I made the resort in record time.

* * *

I remember a very memorable call many years ago while I was still on the helicopter service. This was before we had cellphones. A farm worker was out in the fields on a combine harvester – at least, that's what this city girl thinks it was! Apparently, he had driven over a huge boulder and the blades jammed. Trying to fix it, he climbed onto the back of this huge machine but slipped, landing sideways with one arm jammed in the blades and the other tucked in underneath him. It was quite a long while before someone noticed that the machine wasn't moving.

Let me freeze frame here: one has a maximum of four hours from when a body part is severed from the body to when it has to be reattached. This is obviously feasible in a built-up area like Johannesburg, where you have good hospitals and awesome surgeons. However, in a rural area you can appreciate the enormous obstacles facing both patient and medical team. In our farm worker's case the limb had to be amputated because it was so severely crushed and distorted. When a limb has been severed cleanly, as in a finger that's been sliced off, then it's possible to reattach it. But with a finger that is crushed, as might happen to a person working with a printing press, the actual bones are smashed, which make successful reattachment very unlikely.

Back to our patient. The person who noticed that the harvester had stopped moving climbed into his bakkie and drove out to the field. He got the fright of his life when he saw the situation, and drove to the house to call for medical help. The ambulance finally arrived and had to drive over very rough terrain to get as close as possible to the stricken man. When they assessed what had happened, they realized that not only could they not remove the worker from the machine and its blades, but that he was critical as he had lost a lot of blood. The situation was exacerbated by the heat and the fact that he was not exactly lying down.

They got onto their radio and called for the helicopter. The saving grace here was that there was an excellent handover. They were able to communicate exactly what was needed. Our team therefore arrived with an orthopaedic surgeon who would amputate on scene.

A helicopter displaces as much as three tons of debris when it lifts and when it lands. Also, we had to land as close to the patient as possible and as safely as possible. When we arrived, the man was barely conscious, his poor wife was trying to feed him some sustenance, and the ambulance attendants were looking as pale as he was. He was being propped up by two other people.

We then had the unenviable task of telling the wife as gently as possible that yes, we were going to remove her husband's arm and yes, that is correct Tannie, we would have to remove it there and then; and yes, it is possible and, no, he won't be awake.

I remember very vividly the smell of blood all around us, the barking of two dogs on one of the hakkies nearby, the worried looks on all the faces. I felt the selfless giving of everyone there, as they clamoured to help and hold him upright. You could feel the total unconditional love all around us. I remember the beautiful surroundings in that small part of the field that was this worker's everyday cradle; the field he diligently tended daily, for which he prayed for rain, and knew like the back of his hand; those same fields could have taken his life.

I recall clearly the rank smell of sweat from the men holding their friend up on all sides, mixed with the strong smell of dry earth from the fields around us. Time stood still as we watched the sweat trickling down the face of the surgeon working in the full glare of the afternoon sun. We watched with bated breath, but awe-struck, as his steady hands started to separate the tissue from the blades. I silently acknowledged this was one for the books. I heard his wife being led away and someone saying: "Let us pray." While I assisted the surgeon I remember being so thankful, and so humbled, at being allowed to be a participant on this privileged occasion. Happily, the farm worker spent just a few days in hospital and we last heard he was doing very well.

* * *

Doctors also have wonderful stories to tell. I remember a doctor telling me that while he was on night shift once he was writing up notes on a patient in ICU. The man was hooked up to monitors and a ventilator. The patient's family had arrived to visit him, and they asked the sister why he was so thin.

She explained that he had been in a coma for more than two weeks, and anyone lying still and not using their muscles for any length of time would become thin. The oldest visitor, who was the granny, found it difficult to understand that he was being fed via a tube that went directly to his stomach.

Oblivious to the about-to-unfold drama, the doctor continued to write his notes and paid scant attention to the family. In the meantime the sister had left the ward, and the family was left alone with the patient. Very bad idea.

Soon after, the doctor heard the ventilator alarm screaming. Either the patient had stopped breathing or the machine could not supply the required breaths. He rushed over to find that the family had disconnected the ventilator and were valiantly trying to shove porridge down the airway tube!

Call a policeman

A day that always stands out in my memory was one in which I did a call in Rosettenville. It came in as a double shooting, two policemen in uniform. They were returning from a meeting and noticed a few suspicious-looking characters on the side of the road. As they drove closer the pedestrians opened fire on them. My patient was the driver, a captain with more than 20 years' service, shot in the throat, the bullet exiting through his left shoulder. In minutes my scene was overtaken by policemen. The word was out – two of their senior officers were down.

My patient was not doing well, struggling to breathe as the bullets had passed through his throat, puncturing his lung. We heard that the helicopter had been dispatched and we loaded the patient onto the back of a *bakkie*[20] and made our way to a school rugby field because this was the nearest place to land the helicopter.

I was working that day with Sister Annie Fine, one of my icons. She is a born nursing sister who trained in the Israeli army and takes her oath seriously. I noticed the look in her eye and my heart skipped a beat. I could hear the cardiac monitor screaming that my patient's pulse was deteriorating very quickly. He weakly reached for my hand and pressed it to his chest with the little bit of life left in him. All around us there was bedlam, policemen screaming, various radios going off, the distant sirens of approaching police vans, and the awful, sickly sweet metallic smell of blood. The captain's colleagues were running alongside the bakkie; out of the corner of my eye I could see the helicopter touch down and the flight paramedic rush over. We couldn't have asked for more help – everyone was there – but it was no use, we were losing him.

Again he took my hand, this time pressing it against his left pocket. I realized that he couldn't speak, but wanted me to find something for him. I put my hand into the pocket and took out a photo. It was of him and his wife and a little girl about ten years old. There was no mistaking she was his daughter.

---

20 Small, usually open-backed, utility vehicle

The sound around us was deafening; I'm not sure if it was my own heart that was pounding or his. The cacophony of the helicopter blades, the police radios, the sirens, the shouting, the cardiac monitor – it was like a scene from Dante's *Inferno*. But in a quiet place inside of me I knew as clearly as if he had spoken to me that he wanted me to hold the photo in front of his eyes. I was ashamedly relieved as I hid behind it, and felt the life slowly go out of him. I could almost see the great cross being ticked off in the Book of Life.

There was nothing powerful about it; just incredibly humbling. I felt the lump in my throat rising and obstructing my breathing. The policeman running alongside the *bakkie* was watching me and realized what had happened. He began to swear and suddenly there was a different noise, as if someone had retuned the radio. As the policemen all became aware that their captain had passed away, the sounds changed – angry, raw, very much like standing in the front line of a picketing crowd.

Some of the men just stopped in their tracks as if a switch had been flicked. I could feel the tears starting to form. I placed the photo back in his pocket; I couldn't even look at Annie. I sat down and took a deep breath, trying to dissolve the huge, acrid lump in my throat that had started to burn. I looked at the flight paramedic; no words were needed. He returned to the helicopter to tell the pilot to shut down; some of the policemen were watching us with such scrutiny, I felt like a new virus under a microscope.

The sadness, desperation and anger at the unfairness of it all are always ineffably emotive. I have witnessed this horror many a time and believe me, it never gets better. I still find it difficult to process. This thing of not getting emotionally involved with your patients is utter nonsense. Having a good cry with a patient, feeling and sharing the sadness with family members, doesn't make you forget your dosages, your protocols or how to save a life. I find some of the things I have seen difficult to deal with on an intellectual level, yet I somehow slide into an understanding of it all on another, more emotional level. Almost as if what has just happened makes sense, so that when the moment arrives to tell their family and friends, from somewhere the words come – as if I have the answer to why such a thing should happen.

Because that has to be anathema to all medical professionals – the moment of truth when you have to break the news to the people left behind. It's an interesting fact, borne out by my doctor colleagues – no one is ever taught the art of breaking the bad news properly. They, like me, stumbled and fumbled their way along, learning the hard way. Most of the time, unless it's a gruesome injury, I include the family in the process of resuscitation. This makes the task of breaking the news easier. The truth is there's no right way to do it, each set of circumstances is different.

* * *

I had been into hospital for the third time to have a ganglion on my left wrist removed, and was subsequently placed on light duty. This meant that I was to run the station from the office, for a while. If you are a true Joburger, you will love the Highveld nights, her sounds and smells. Sounds like sirens and car alarms make a kind of music of their own; and I love the sound of frogs, not to mention those wonderful summer storms. I'm sure it's not quite as spectacular as sitting on your stoep in the Little Karoo, slicing biltong and drinking *moerkoffie*[21], but the Highveld nights have a special beauty that is all their own. People can walk around wearing vests, listening to the crickets and watching the

---

21 A traditional South African coffee made from roasted coffee beans placed in a muslin bag and brewed in a tin coffee pot

geckos catching moths, with car alarms and bullfrogs competing for sound space in the background.

On one lovely summer night, I was at the Brixton station playing duty officer. It was a busy night and the station was empty except for Frankie, a very old ambulance attendant. He didn't work on the road any more but was responsible for filling the oxygen cylinders. The Brixton station is across the road from the Westpark cemetery. I was sitting in the office reading Rose Madder, my favorite Stephen King story, when I heard a very loud and distinct snorting sound.

At first I ignored it and continued reading. Then I heard it again. I'm not sure if it's years of working in Hillbrow that makes you lose all sense of fear or just my small-woman-syndrome attitude, but I put down my book and ventured out towards the noise. I looked out over the top of the stable door and saw nothing that could be making that sound. I called Frankie on the public address system.

He arrived a few minutes later and it was obvious I had woken him up. As I was about to explain the strange sound, we both heard it. This time it sounded as if it was in the office. I looked out of the door again and came face to face with a real live pig. Frankie almost jumped onto the filing cabinet.

I stared at this porker, who was quite a size. It stared back at me, and then it wandered around the parade ground sniffing in our dustbins. Being a city girl, I don't do pigs. But I knew if the pig headed towards the main road that runs past Garden City Clinic, it could cause a complete catastrophe.

I got onto the radio and requested backup. I realized what an ass I must have sounded like. They were wondering if they'd heard correctly at the other end. Please repeat – what kind of backup did I say I needed? I carefully repeated my message, and then spelled it out.

"I have a Papa India Golf running around the station and we need to corner it before something happens to it."

After a long silence, the jokes started: how long before breakfast, was there enough bacon to go round, with apologies to the Muslim and Jewish medics because they would miss out. Within a few minutes I had the cavalry at the station; we had traffic police, tow-truck guys and ambulances.

We then discovered that the Police Headquarters up the road kept a farmyard and someone had left the gate open. The fun began as uniformed personnel tried to corner the pig. The poor creature was scared spitless from all the swearing, shouting, laughing and bright star-bar lights – and promptly bolted into the cemetery. Running after it, like in the story of the gingerbread man, was an assortment of uniformed men and a woman, gesticulating madly because it was then headed towards the Muslim section. It looked like something out of a Carry On movie.

They finally managed to coax the pig back into the parade ground and closed the gate. I, naturally, was shouting suggestions and delegating duties safely from the other side of the stable door.

At one stage they had a spine board leaning as a ramp into one of the police vans. As Babe was being persuaded to walk the plank it broke in two, and then all hell broke loose. The pig had seriously lost its sense of humour by now, the crews had run out of jokes, and I was already thinking about the major paperwork I would have to come up with to explain how a spine board was broken by a pig. Then followed strategies and summit meetings for the pig's D-day, with suggestions ranging from throwing a blanket over him to the interesting but risky "let's shock him".

However, all's well that ends well; Babe was captured and sent back to his paddock in the farmyard. Everyone thanked me for the great time – as if I had deliberately organized it – and the crews all left to go and save some more lives, making jokes about having bacon and eggs for breakfast.

* * *

I was once called to a shooting in the centre of town. The story I was told was that, after a robbery, the police shot at the getaway car and a bullet entered the back window and struck one of the robbers in the head. I arrived at the scene and it was very evident from the amount of brain matter on the inside roof of the car that this man was dead. Puzzled, I asked the policeman in charge where the patient was, thinking I had missed something.

He looked at me like I was dim and told me to please treat the patient sitting in the back seat. I looked at him and was about to ask him to repeat himself, but judging by the look on his face he was clearly not going to. I told him that the man was dead; he argued with me that the patient was sitting upright and his eyes were open.

Time for that all-important part of my job – public education. I walked over to the patient, closed his eyes and gently moved him from the vertical to the horizontal ... the cop looked incredulously at me and said "eish!"

* * *

Staying on the subject of cops, there are many calls I remember, some for sheer stupidity and others for the absolute respect engendered, for what they are subjected to. They have to endure their fair share of abuse from the public – and let's not forget the Bystanders!

One afternoon I was called to Hillbrow Hospital to a shooting in a ward. Now this is not as unusual as it sounds because there are occasions in gang fights when the oppressors or the oppressed arrive en masse in casualty to finish off the job. That's why Johannesburg Hospital looks like Fort Knox these days. I arrived at casualty and was informed that the patient was in the intensive care ward. I asked why they had sent for me then, and got no answer. I was promptly escorted by a policeman wearing an important-looking uniform and a serious, dead-pan expression. The patient was a recovering suspect who had been doing well and, in fact, was to be taken off the respirator that day. When the policeman who was guarding him arrived for a change of shift, the two cops sat down and exchanged small talk. And then for some reason one cop slid his pistol across the bedside table and, in so doing, a round went off, entered one side of the patient's chest and exited through the other side, killing him instantly and luckily just missing the patient in the bed next to him. Did I mention that the patient had been doing so well? Interesting story, but one cop's career was reset to zero.

* * *

9

Some things remain a mystery

I can't deny that in our field of work we see the most incredible things. Things that would make Einstein rethink his theory of relativity.

A large percentage of the hundreds of people who are killed in motor accidents daily in South Africa, are pedestrians. Sadly, many people have to walk fair distances to their nearest local shop or café, and they often have to cross a busy road. If it's a highway, it becomes an exceedingly dangerous exercise. It's difficult to judge the distance between speeding cars and at night the perspective becomes almost impossible. Added to that, many of these people have fuelled themselves with a bit of alcohol and are convinced they have super powers.

This means that in almost all cases, pedestrians on highways are usually dead by the time you reach them, or are very seriously injured. There is usually no in-between, given the speed of the cars. So when I was called to attend to a pedestrian on the N1 concrete highway in the early hours of the morning, I didn't hold out much hope.

When I arrived at the given spot, looking for the victim, I saw a woman standing next to an older model Mazda talking on her cellphone. I drove right past her, but saw nothing further on. I reversed, stopped next to her and got out. I asked her if she had called for an ambulance. Looking idly at her car, I got quite a shock when I saw that the entire front windscreen was missing. I walked around the car and saw that the back windscreen was also gone. Furthermore, there was a baby strapped in behind the driver's seat, and the baby's minder sitting next to it.

I asked her if she was sure she had struck a pedestrian. She vigorously confirmed this. "Oh yes, I'm absolutely sure. It's not exactly the kind of thing one could make up! How on earth do you think I broke the windscreens?"

She said she'd seen him stepping out in front of her at the last second, adding that he had been wearing a light-coloured jacket.

Usually in this type of accident, the pedestrian folds over the bonnet of the car, unless the vehicle is high like a taxi or a bus.

The front passenger is normally the one to be injured as the pedestrian hurtles through the windscreen – having approached from the driver's side and misjudged the speed of the vehicle.

By this time the highway patrol had arrived and we went over the story again. It seemed unfathomable that a body could travel dead centre, between the headrests and the limited space between the roof and the seats – and then exit. It just wasn't possible. Luckily, the baby's nanny had been sleeping on the back seat.

The traffic officer and I exchanged rueful looks. What the lady was telling us seemed quite impossible. However, there was nothing to lose by going over the ground, and we had to solve the mystery. So, although we both thought it was pointless, the traffic officer and I walked behind the car for a few metres.

Incredibly, sure enough, there he was! He was wearing a light-colored jacket, and had no recognizable head.

* * *

Another instance illustrating the unbelievable is one that I remember distinctly. I was still a basic ambulance attendant in my second year. It was in the very early hours of a Sunday morning, following a rather busy night. It had started drizzling. My partner, Johan, was a gentle man who used to knit for relaxation. He was teased mercilessly but I adored him and we worked well together. We understood one another and knew each other's weaknesses and strengths. Whenever it was quiet, we would sit together in the ambulance, and wait. I always had my nose in a book and he would be knitting.

I knew he was also gay, and he was easy to share stories with.

"How do your parents handle your being homosexual?" I asked him that dark morning as we sat in the vehicle.

"Not very well. I was brought up in a strict, religious home." He paused between a purl and a plain stitch. "My father was a church elder. What about yours?"

"Mine also can't accept it. They're both Italian, from the old school. My father believes I should be in the kitchen – and look like Sophia Loren." This remark made us both scream with laughter.

"Oh God, I love her," he said, "Just love those big sunglasses she wears."

"So you should, you're a screaming queen, and that kind of appreciation is the first sign of being gay," I replied.

"Surely our parents should have seen we were heading that way? Did you play with motor cars?" he asked.

"No, not really. I was given dolls and I used to cut them open, stuff their stomachs with stuff, and get my little brother to help me with surgery."

We laughed comfortably together, happy members of the 'pink shift'.

So there we were that early morning. We decided to go back to the station to get more disposable equipment and on the way we drove past a large BMW parked on the side of the road in a space that was as large as a garage. As we passed, I looked at the face of the man in the driver's seat, and his expression struck me as very odd. The situation needed to be investigated. Besides, having such an expensive car, why would he be out so late and not in his equally expensive bed? The only other logical conclusion was that he was getting a blow job, but that was not a spot that was known for that kind of thing. It was too close to both the residential areas and the main road.

I asked Johan to stop so I could see what was happening. He said I should leave it alone, but obligingly stopped as he knew I wouldn't give in quietly. I got out and approached the vehicle. The man was still sitting very still, holding the steering wheel with a puzzled expression on his face. We are taught to approach a door or a situation from the side if we feel unsure. I started talking loudly, hoping he would look in my direction as there was virtually no light to see him properly. By this time I was right alongside the vehicle and saw the window was slightly open.

I informed him in my best authoritarian manner that I was going to put my arm in his window and open the door. He didn't answer me. I remember my brain racing, wondering if at any minute he would say "Boo – got you!" or climax and I would come face to face with some lady of the night. Because of the poor lighting I placed my mini maglight in my mouth and opened the door. Still he didn't move. I reached out for his neck and felt for a pulse. I began swearing loudly.

I yelled for Johan to call for back-up as we had a resuscitation on our hands; he swore louder than I did. I leaned over the man to undo his safety belt and then I noticed the reason why he was sitting so still.

He had managed to drive over a lamppost. The post had entered the floor of the car in the front, had come through the floorboards between the pedals and run parallel to the steering column and then – horribly, unthinkably – come up through the seat so that he was literally skewered like a human kebab. It took us more than three hours to get him out of there.

* * *

There are times in this job when the feeling of unreality becomes so strong that one wouldn't flinch at the strangest happenings. Sometimes I expect Salvador Dali to pop in and smile while he tweaks his curly moustache, accompanied by Barry Manilow elevator music playing in the background. I would accept it as being quite normal.

A number of medics do voluntary work at various places like the Johannesburg General Hospital, or Baragwaneth, or any of the busy casualties where one is exposed to a lot of trauma. It's excellent training as one learns very quickly, mostly by being thrown in at the deep end because it's not unusual to work with skeleton staff.

On one particular evening we were 'rocking' in casualty at Joburg Gen. The beds were all occupied, blood on the floor, files piling up on the counter, stocks running low, tempers high – helped along by bad coffee – and the sympathy level was below zero. I had just finished suturing a patient who'd sustained a large laceration on his head caused by a bottle being thrown out of a building in Hillbrow.

There is a weird phenomenon in Hillbrow; the people who live there – all in high-rise buildings – adhere to a very entrenched and strange tradition. They spend the year accumulating all their electrical

129

appliances that don't work, and any other object that would ordinarily be dumped at the junkyard. These all end up on their balconies.

Then, come New Year's Eve they indulge themselves. They take supreme pleasure in throwing the offending objects like missiles, at some poor, unsuspecting but probably inebriated individual who happens to be silly enough to walk around on the street below without a helmet.

On this day, as I finished cleaning the sutured wound, we heard the emergency helicopter come in. I discharged my patient and proceeded to the resuscitation bay to help out.

The patient was a young man who had tried to commit suicide by leaning on his double-barrelled shotgun, placing his thumb on the trigger. The result was that his face was blown off at an oblique angle, leaving a partial left ear, no right eye, and a partially open left cranium. I was on the right side of him and the doctor asked me to run another intravenous line on his right arm.

There must have been six to eight people in that room all trying to prolong the life of what was left of this human being. If you have ever seen the movie The Fly, that is what came to mind when you looked at him; his injuries were horrendous. As I came closer to him to place the needle in his vein he straightened his arm. I remember the entire room becoming silent as if someone had turned the sound off. Time stood still. I was conscious of everybody holding their breath – every medically trained person stared at him in utter disbelief.

When the doctor managed to regain his composure he leaned close to what was left of the patient's ear and asked him if he could hear him. Whatever was left of his brain matter managed to process the info and he slowly and grotesquely nodded his head. He was stabilized, and rushed to theatre where he was worked on by various surgeons. I heard later that he did not survive. We talked about that for many months.

* * *

Yes, you guessed it – it's night shift again. I'm driving around admiring the city, coffee in polystyrene container, doing a responsible 40 km an hour. I'm coming over the bridge in Killarney that separates the Wilds from inner Killarney. There is another bridge a little lower down, which runs parallel to it. I notice a sports model Mercedes parked with the top down and no one in it. I have only my coffee to finish, so I drive slowly to it. I see no one around (sound familiar?) drive past, make a u-turn and return. I get out and walk over (again, sound familiar?). There is no one. Not a sausage. But I do notice that there is a photo album and a few letters on the passenger seat. What really piques my curiosity is that the keys are still in the ignition. Silly man – doesn't he know he's in Joburg; someone could kill him just for the album.

I wait, most intrigued by all of this. It is just me, the car, the night, and my coffee. The only sound – the passing cars below me on the M1 South. I decide to peek at the photos. They are of a family at the seaside; pictures of some huge machinery being lifted by a crane; and some of concrete being poured. I occupy myself with conspiracy theories. Here's my first: he has wiped out his family and, to avoid the papers exposing his sordid affair with his Phillipino domestic worker, he has used the huge machinery in the photos to bury them in concrete.

I wait a while longer – the 'killer' has not materialized. Reluctantly I get on the radio and report in. I can just imagine the scenario in that SAP control room whenever that particular call comes in saying "a paramedic has found an abandoned car ...".

I bet the first thing they say is: "Don't tell me, she's a shorty, works alone, has grey hair and is scared of nothing."

By the time they arrive, no killer has shown up yet. It is now about 4 am, some people are already walking to work. The cops have called the dog squad in; we surmise that perhaps he might be hiding in the embankment amongst those big green ivy leaves – which are home to so many Park Town prawns. Time to make an exit in case they ask me to wade through said underbrush, but not before an honest policeman asks, "Why didn't you just take the car? No one would ever have found out." Silly man, doesn't he watch CSI? They'll shine their mini maglights and find me by simply punching a few buttons in a machine that is housed in a very uberchic glass office and all my up-to-date details would appear.

My shift ends at 6 am and there is still no sign of the 'killer'. I later find out that the missing man parked his car, got out to have a pee and fell down the embankment. These things happen when one is fall-down drunk.

He was smacked by a car on the highway below, much earlier in the evening, and ended up in the Johannesburg Hospital. He was extremely lucky his car was untouched. And the meaning of the photo album? One of Life's Great Mysteries – I'm still working on it.

* * *

I had an odd experience at Bruma Lake many years ago, long before the market and shops creating Asian City were built. Answering a call, I arrived and found a Volkswagen Beetle had gone through the wooden fence that bordered the street and on to the grassy area. There had been two young people in the car – a man and a woman. She was lying across the two front seats and he was outside, lying next to the front right wheel. He was unconscious, badly hurt and had a severely fractured right arm.

When the young woman began stirring, and finally came to, I examined her, and asked her who had been driving. She wouldn't answer me. An ambulance had already been dispatched, and while we made our way back to the road where it would collect the patients, she showed signs of great agitation, asking constantly whether I'd seen her blue denim tog bag. She insisted it must be found and brought to her;

she wasn't going anywhere without it. While the young man was being put onto a stretcher, I discovered it, picked it up and we all went off to the hospital. She still refused to divulge who had been driving.

At the hospital we handed the patients over and I fetched the blue bag. I had a strange feeling about it, so insisted that other people be present when it was opened. With two nursing sisters watching, I opened the bag – and found that it was filled with money tied in neat bundles. We immediately called the police, and in the presence of a policeman we counted the money. There was a total of R270 000 and three handguns – like something straight out of a Martin Scorsese movie! I made copious notes as I had a feeling that wasn't going to be the last I'd hear of it.

Sure enough, about three years later I got a call from an insurance company. Did I remember the event, and who was driving? If I could prove the driver was the male involved, he would receive a huge payout as he lost his right arm.

I told the caller that I didn't know who the driver was, as the information was never given. Then began a period when I became afraid to answer my phone. First there were enticing bribes – if I said the man had been driving, I would be well recompensed. When I didn't fall for that, they began threatening me. I eventually had to change my cell number.

* * *

One of my favourite stories was told on the radio and although I feel a bit as if I'm digressing, it's such a great story it deserves to be retold. And it's a true story – not an urban legend.

A woman went to do her monthly shopping; it was a hot day and she deposited all the bags on the back shelf in her little Golf. She had parked in front of a dry cleaning shop and was about to start her car when an almighty bang went off and she felt a weight against her head. She instantly left the ignition, sat bolt upright and proceeded to hold her head together, feeling her brain matter oozing out between her fingers. She dared not even reach for the cellphone in case she bled more or lost consciousness ... Two hours later the owner of the dry cleaner noticed this woman was still in that 'bugger of a migraine' position and decided to go out to investigate.

He asked her if she was okay. She replied, "I have been shot in the head, please can you call for an ambulance." The man flew off faster than you can say Organ Donor. On arrival the ambulance crew noticed that she was still holding her head, stemming the flow of 'blood.'

It transpired that a canister among her groceries, containing ready-made dough, had been facing the back of her head; the build-up of heat inside the car caused the missile to explode, striking the back of her head. The poor woman was convinced she had sustained a serious gunshot to the head, which was particularly convincing as she felt the warm, doughy 'brain matter' sliding down the back of her head. Personally, if that had been me, I would have emigrated.

* * *

Sometimes one becomes unsure of whether things really happened, or whether urban legend has taken over. One of those stories, which I've heard but never saw personally, was the story about patients who kept dying in a certain bed in a certain ward. More strange was the fact that they continued to die on a particular day. After the intelligentsia were called in, they did one of those CSI scenarios, with photos on the wall, flowcharts, low lighting, tense mood, loads of coffee and even more knitted eyebrows.

They planned to stay around the offending bed and stake it out; no-one came into the ward who was not allowed to, and yet, the respirator

134

alarm went off! They all rushed in – to be confronted by a cleaner clasping the plug for the respirator as she was about to swap it for the vacuum cleaner plug!!

10

Where the job can take you

WHEN I began writing this book, I had started working abroad and was doing a locum on a gold mine in Tanzania. My career has taken me to wonderful places – Chioggia in Italy, Bergen in Norway, French Guyana, Surinam, Dar es Salaam, and Stornoway; Ulsan in South Korea, Dubai, Singapore, Madagascar and Angola – in fact, to 77 towns in 28 countries when I last checked.

I have had the privilege of living in hotels near the docks where ships are built, learning about the ways of the people, and eating their food. It has made me realize that we are all very much alike; the same things make us laugh. We all complain about taxes and taxis; and we all love ragging our friends from other countries about their funny beliefs, their strange food and the way they speak. And I still find it strange that some people eat live little fish in cabbage leaves, yet they find it bizarre that we eat biltong.

Something I found fascinating in the hotels in Korea was that the hotel rooms are fitted with a lifeline. This is essential for emergency exits when a typhoon hits the building, an ever-present possibility. It takes the form of a hook on the wall closest to the balcony outside; below it is a suitcase containing a type of nappy and a lifeline cable. When a crisis happens, you attach the cable around your waist, hook it onto the special hook in the wall, and then lower yourself – presumably to safety.

In Madagascar I watched as the locals drank the water that rice is cooked in as a beverage they considered far superior to coffee. I have lived and worked in parts of Luanda that are more dangerous than Johannesburg on a Saturday night at month end. I have overcome my fear of snakes in remote areas of the world; I have woken up in my cabin on oil rigs and at night watched the most spectacular sunsets as the evening sky gently melted into the horizon. I have worked on survey vessels in the North Sea and have been called in the middle of the night by the marine mammal observers on board to see a dead whale float past the ship. The sight of such a majestic creature on top of the water, beneath a full moon, still gives me goosebumps.

In the North Sea the currents are so rough that fellow crew members take their mattresses off their beds and lie on the floor because they grow tired of hanging onto the sides of the bed. I have witnessed seas so rough that I held my breath as I watched a fax machine that was bolted to a desk, which was bolted to the floor panels, fly out of its moorings. I have watched with a full heart as dolphins and enormous stingrays played alongside an oil rig, reminding us that we are very privileged to be sharing their space.

I have sat in galleys and eaten with so many different crew members from all over the world that it felt like I was breaking bread with the League of Nations. I have watched birds land on the deck of a survey vessel off the Norwegian coast, and been told that these little birds flew all the way from Nigeria. I have held geckos that look as if lichen has grown on them, whose touch is as gentle as a new-born baby's. Standing in awe, I have watched old women bent from lives of hardship, carry loads many times their own weight and still manage a toothless grin. I have smelled the two fish sold on the side of the road by a mother, with children on her back in the searing Tanzanian sun; I've trembled, watching eight-metre waves crash over the deck of our boat outside Surinam.

In Tanzania I repaired holes in fences in a camp where the expats lived; holes made by locals who come in at night and steal small rocks left after blasting to take home and crush by hand to try and extract gold. On incomparable Madagascar, I held a beautiful lemur in the palm of my hand, one of many that had to be relocated because man is deforesting their home to make way for a mine. I have looked on as mothers carry babies on their backs and walk barefoot over the most impossible terrain, all the while chatting to each other as unconcernedly as western women do in a shopping mall.

I once really frightened the people in a very remote village when I opened my mouth to speak. They had never seen orthodontic braces before! There are still little villages where time seems to have stood still. Like Stornoway, where there is a law stating that shops may not have neon light displays hanging outside, as it detracts from the beauty of the buildings.

Working in Luanda, I watched from a bus at night how people disappear into the storm-water drains to bed down for the night. I have had the privilege of working at Porto Amboimo in Angola, so remote that every evening and on Sundays we would all go fishing on a beach where there were no other human beings.

I've tasted reindeer, stingray, sand shark and gimpap (South Korean type sushi).

And think how much poorer my life would have been had I not had the fun of being taught how to steer monster trucks and cranes – all five feet of me!

I've seen pathology I'd never heard of in patients, and watched in fascination how locals treat it. I will never forget looking into the eyes of children who were completely poverty-stricken and hungry; and yet were still able to laugh from deep inside, smile their inner smiles and play in the dirty, dusty streets, their grubby fingers waving me on.

I have been blessed to record these images on my own retinas first rather than merely reading about them in books. The strongest feeling I have about it all is one of great humility.

* * *

As an ALS paramedic there are many options available because you can leave the country and be snapped up by companies who specialise in remote-site paramedic work. These sites can be on land or offshore.

Out in the bundu

Sometimes the site you're sent to is well established with a clinic, or there may be nothing there because they've only just started making roads and establishing a camp for the client's enterprise. This could be the beginnings of a gold, platinum or nickel mine, a survey site for testing water or sand, where clients survey the soil to find a suitable site to build large structures or mines. When the site is established but has no clinic, the medic does an assessment of what is needed. This depends on the number of expats working on that site, the distance to the nearest hospital, and the infrastructure of the resources available to both the client and the medic.

A good example of an established site is the Geita gold mine in Tanzania, which is the third largest gold mine in the world. There are more than 2 000 people on this site. Geita has a mini hospital, with facilities such as X-rays and blood laboratories.

I currently work at a similar mine in Guinea, West Africa. We have a hospital and clinic with a small team of doctors and nurses who are responsible for more than 2 000 people. I head up the emergency services division and am responsible for all emergency medical training. I am also the first responder for all medical emergencies, which means that I am on call 24 hours a day, seven days a week for the duration of my 3–3.5 month shift. Working here has opened my eyes. The country is predominantly Muslim, so many traditions that govern everyday life also govern life on site and in the hospital. For instance, by 12 pm the hospital resembles a ghost town – all the female patients who are mobile scurry off home to make food for the men. I was also introduced to 'fatigue rest', a totally foreign concept here in South Africa. Quite simply, if a staff member feels 'fatigued', they can request some respite and you are obliged to allow them up to four hours to rest or sleep, wherever you can find them a spot. It could be a spare hospital bed, a chair, even the back seat of a vehicle! It's quite a miracle that anything gets done. One also sees things you would never see in a travel guide, such as a cow who has been fitted with a paint bucket over her snout as punishment simply because she's eaten grass in the wrong field, or cars with six people sitting on the roof, three on each side, resting their feet on the window ledge for extra comfort as they hurtle past on their way to do illegal mining!

Interestingly, I had been on the Guinea site for just one month when the West African Ebola crisis broke out – the one that went global – and we were smack bang in the middle of it! I was tasked with setting up an isolation ward, protocols, and everything that was needed to contain the virus and prevent it from entering our camp. I'm a paramedic –

I am comfortable with blood, screaming ECG machines, drunk and obnoxious patients and drug dosages. I was clueless though when it came to setting up an isolation ward and protocols. The angels were on my side: we had a locum doctor from South Africa who was well versed in this who assisted me, and we pulled it together. Much reading and research took place at night, and strict protocols were discussed and argued over. Security guards no longer just guarded the camp; they now took temperatures of every person coming into the camp. Bus drivers, too, did double duty by taking the temperatures of every person climbing onto a bus. Cleaners no longer just cleaned floors – like a little recognisance squad, every bus was sprayed before anyone sat down; and for every vehicle that came through the gate, the driver had to lean out the window while his or her hands were sprayed with chlorinated water and their temperature was taken. All passengers had to get out of their vehicles and walk through the turnstiles to wash their hands and have their temperatures taken. Anyone with a temperature over 37.8°C was taken aside. A special ambulance picked them up, took them to the hospital via the back route, and they were put into a ward where they were tested for malaria as most fevers during that time were malaria-related. Fortunately, we did not have a single Ebola case in our camp.

Unlike the Guinea site I work on now, some of the sites I have worked on have not needed a hospital because there were no more than 50 expats; a small medical facility was therefore ample.

On the smaller sites, the medic works alone. Most of the time you see primary healthcare patients with coughs, colds, and stomach troubles. And you are there, of course, for all sorts of trauma work, from suturing wounds, lancing boils and syringing ears, to the airlifting of a patient in critical condition to the nearest hospital.

* * *

Being away from home has a few advantages when you work in a remote area in Africa. The biggest bonus is no traffic congestion because we live where we work. If you're one of those with a Born-to-Shop sticker on your car, you won't survive. There are very few shops and those that there are don't sell one tenth of the basic stuff we take for granted back home. The next person who tells me that South Africa is like any other African state will be sent to ICU, and it won't be an overnight stay. You only have to land in any of our big airports and you know you're in a first-world country.

* * *

For one of my assignments I had my own cabin on the beach! This was in Pemba, Mozambique. It came with two beds, two steel cupboards and essential aircon. I would walk about 10 metres to the showers. The water was a bit salty as we pumped it directly from the sea and the pump was a bit dysfunctional. Still, the view was awesome and provided a welcome end to my working day.

My typical day would start at 5.45 am. I'd join the guys for breakfast, which consisted of either cornflakes or that delicious but evil Portuguese bread that would land directly on my hips. Then I'd be off to my clinic to answer emails and sort out office admin; keeping tabs on stock, reordering the necessaries, and Skyping friends. We had a proper coffee machine and every morning I'd kick-start my day with a decent espresso. What can I say, I'm Italian.

Then I'd do weekly inspections of the camp, kitchen, eating facilities, washroom bays – assessing the general hygiene. In between this there were occasional patients, as I practised mostly primary health care there, dispensing medication and seeing the occasional injury on duty, suturing wounds and giving vaccinations.

I was primarily there in the event of something major happening, as in a traumatic injury where the patient needed urgent medical intervention as we were miles from the nearest hospital. Expats were covered by medical insurance and they received excellent care; it was up to the medic to keep them alive, stabilize them and evacuate them off site by either helicopter or fixed wing. Most expats working in Africa will be flown to South Africa and treated there, if necessary, as South Africa definitely still has the best medical facilities.

I'd also give first-aid training to the fire team guys, and do presentations if and when the need arose. For instance, if I saw an outbreak of diarrhoea in the camp, I would give a short lecture on hand washing, transmission of germs, and so on. I would also do walks around the camp, checking that people wore the personal protective equipment they were issued with, making sure that they were drinking enough water, and lecturing them about the importance of wearing sunscreen. If they were being remiss about it, I'd rub it on them myself. I saw them as 'my boys' and you could see they loved it.

On weekends I frequented a wonderful restaurant in town that served great food and I quickly became friends with the South African chef there, Tinus. It was an assignment where life felt a little 'normal' and, thanks to Tinus's company on his days off, I experienced some quality of life whilst on the job as we walked, chatted, swam, and idled our spare hours away. Tinus and I have remained friends to this day.

*　*　*

When I worked in Angola, I started my day at 4:55 am. For security reasons, no-one is allowed to walk anywhere, so the bus would pick us up at 5.15 am. Because it could be unsafe, especially for Westerners, we were driven everywhere.

The working day ended at 6:30 pm, when it was back to your hotel room until the next morning. There was no such thing as a day off, and the highlight was Thursday when we were taken to the supermarket to buy our groceries for dinner, as it was the only meal not provided.

Most of us lived on tuna and beans out of cans as those were regarded as safe. The base is situated at the harbour and is surrounded by fine, powdery red sand, and everywhere there is evidence of poverty.

The local people throw their waste into a huge canal that leads directly into the sea. This means that when the rains come, the sand is broken down virtually into faecal matter. Not exactly health-promoting.

The hotel room and its four walls becomes your home for the next six weeks. A lot of the men get silly; they haven't heard of 'helping themselves' and stupidly bring prostitutes to their rooms, then wonder why they get cleaned out. There are very strict rules within companies about this sort of risky behaviour – it can mean instant dismissal because it endangers the lives of everyone else in the hotel.

The simplest things we take completely for granted back home are a huge mission to accomplish in most parts of Africa. One cannot, for instance, just go out and buy a magazine as there are no shops that sell them – so you have to rely on colleagues bringing back the newspaper from home to catch up on local news. Other than that, you can watch the latest on CNN or SKY news.

* * *

Thanks to social media and cellphones, news travels very quickly. Even in war zones and areas of unrest. Before I joined the Guinea site, I was working for a medical support company in Mogadishu, Somalia, which at the time was frequently in the news because of all the bombs that were going off amidst clashes between Al-Shabab and the Somalian armed forces.

Now this is not a place for those of nervous disposition or who are easily offended. I say this because, from the time you land, you are assaulted by smells, sights and sounds that are unforgettable, to say the least. When you receive your ticket to fly on the notorious Mogadishu

Express, you get *just* a ticket, *not* a seat number. You can be forgiven for becoming suddenly disoriented when, as the gates open, there is an urgent mass exodus through one door, as if the Somalian Civil War were right behind you. If that were not enough to frighten you, then how about the fact that you board the plane at the back via a small, one person ladder? All the Fatimas and Aishas in different hijabs bustle for position, much like in a rugby scrum, and they usually have four-and-a-half kids in tow who are already used to this dance.

Finally, you find yourself seated next to a Somalian who keeps staring at you, and then you notice it – a fly! Yes, in all my years of travelling, not a single aeroplane had flies clocking up voyager miles on the same flight as me. And forget the customary airline food; you get a small, wrapped slice of sponge cake and a choice of water or coke. Thats it!

Upon arrival at the airport, the war begins. Not the war outside the green zone where Al-Shabab is fighting the Somalis, but the war of getting through customs and obtaining your precious luggage. First, you are herded into a room. Tradition dictates that your luggage is kicked down a concrete slope into this room, and a few airport workers fetch the disheveled luggage and place it in three neat rows. Then all hell breaks loose as everyone yells and shouts and tries to make eye contact with the luggage officials to pass them their luggage. But the pièce de résistance is when the main luggage official – an old man dressed in an even older army uniform and wielding a stick – sharply whacks any passenger who dares to lean over to try and grab their luggage. No one is safe – not men, women nor children! Anywhere else in the world, assaulting passengers in this way would result in a hearing and a dismissal. In Mogadishu, this is just another day at the airport.

While in Mogadishu, I worked at the military camp located inside the green zone (safe zone) next to the airport, as well as another site in the city centre that fell outside the green zone. To get to the city site, we had to don full protective gear – helmet and bulletproof vests – and travel in hot, armoured vehicles in a security convoy. The reality of war is so very different to the reality of working in Hillbrow. The Hillbrow animal is predictable, even if they are on coke. In a country where war is raging, people are paid 20USD to let off a grenade in a market place. They do this not because they are terrorists, but because they are desperate for money. The face of the enemy is impossible to profile.

The day they stormed the UN offices[22] situated less than 50 metres from our compound, was unforgettable; the explosion was like nothing I'd ever experienced before. It was followed by gun fire, which continued for over an hour as the brave Somali soldiers kept the terrorists away from the building. The shrapnel that flew over our compound wall made it all very real. The Somali soldiers are like nothing you'd expect as far as soldiers are concerned. They don't have camouflage outfits, voice-activated radios, infra-red glasses, or fancy backpacks. Instead, they are dressed in long flowing robes, wear flip flops, and chew a lot of Khat[23] to keep them awake. They can sleep on the ground with no mat, and despite their appearance, are as tough as can be. We huddled in the corridor with our helmets and bulletproof vests awaiting our private security to give us instructions, but being in a compound you are a sitting duck. One cannot but marvel at the age of cellphones, as exactly 11 minutes after the explosion, the first news broke through the major online news outlets and we had regular updates on what was happening on the other side of our wall.

* * *

---

22   At least 15 people, including four foreigners, were killed on 19 June 2013 in an assault by militant Islamists on the UN office in Mogadishu, the Somalian capital.

23   Khat – used as a stimulant – is a flowering plant native to the Horn of Africa and the Arabian Peninsula. Khat chewing is a social custom dating back thousands of years.

On a much lighter note, many years ago when working in Luanda, I was running a clinic at a spooling base[24]. A patient walked in complaining of feeling nauseous. I gave him medication. A little later he returned – he was still complaining of nausea. I thought to myself, well he can't be faking not wanting to work as he is on management level, and also I've never seen him in my clinic before, so he's not a regular.

I gave him more medication for nausea and he left. Sure enough, a while later he was back. I was now getting concerned. I told him the only alternative left was a suppository or an injection, because nothing seemed to stay in his stomach long enough. I felt sure he would refuse a suppository because men really don't like those things. Surprise, surprise – he said he would take the suppository, and left. I thought it strange, but was pleasantly surprised. About 20 minutes later he returned and was looking rather green. And sorry for himself. And sweating. I told him to lie down while I phoned my back-up doctor for advice. While I was on the phone in the corner I saw him gesticulating wildly – he urgently needed to vomit. So, in a well-practised move I handed him the bowl and continued talking to the doctor while he was hurling his guts out. I finished on the phone and walked over to him to take his blood pressure, and happened (like any good paramedic) to look at the vomit. I noticed a brownish liquid (probably coffee) and then I saw it, a little whitish torpedo-type thingy floating in the vomited contents. I confirmed with him that he had not eaten anything. He told me earnestly: "I swear doctor, I ate nothing, and the last thing

---

24 A spooling base is a section of the harbour set aside for a gas or oil company, where the pipes that are laid on the seabed to carry oil or gas are welded together and wound around a huge wheel. The welding is carefully X-rayed for defects or weaknesses before being subjected to the pressure inside the pipes and the sea outside.

I swallowed was the suppository you gave me twenty minutes ago."
Three cheers for the day shift.

* * *

When I worked in Porto Amboimo, which is about 300 km south of
Luanda, I arrived back on shift after six weeks off to find a brand-new
arrival – Bok, who was a black, baby goat who had wandered into
our camp with the placenta still attached and no mother to be seen.
Everybody loved Bok. The HSE[25] Manager, Darrel, took her under his
wing and fed her five times a day out of a bottle. She had a special foam
mattress next to his desk in his office and as soon as he went out the
door, she would cry for him.

When we work on the rigs, we have a rotation schedule of six weeks
duty, followed by six weeks at home. When Darrel had to go home –
who was left to look after Bok? You got it, yes, me! Now I am a city
girl, I know squat about goats and even less about their strange habits.
We also had a dog, Tess, on site who belonged to the camp boss and
his wife. The loveliest friendship developed between Tess and Bok;
they were inseparable. At night Tess would catch large crabs and Bok
would stand on the sidelines silently cheering her on. In the evening
the camp boss would go for a walk escorted by Bok and Tess. She also
accompanied us to the beach. The poor goat had an identity crisis; she
really thought she was a dog.

At night, Bok had to sleep with me, and so began a strange bedtime
ritual. I would have dinner while Bok stood outside the dining area,
knocking on the glass door with her hooves. Then it was time for her
dinner. After that we enjoyed a few hours around the campfire and then

---

25   Health, Safety and Environment

to bed, where the fun began. I would change into my jimmies as Bok, the voyeur, watched me. Now, as I've mentioned before, I'm strictly a city girl and there are some things I'm just not used to. Have you ever looked a goat in the eye? They have a vertical iris, which makes them seem at times to be bordering on evil. Then I would lie down with my book, and wait. On cue, Bok would jump onto my bed, watch me for a few seconds then lie down with her head in the crook of my right arm. This would have been very cute except that goats are not the softest of animals. Add to that the fact that they are ruminants! I still don't understand why you would chew when there is nothing in your mouth! She refused to lie on the floor and insisted on sharing my bed; eventually I compromised and lay head to foot with her.

Then promptly at 3 am every morning, Bok would wake up, jump off the bed and decide it was time to play. Being jolted out of sleep by the sound of loud hooves on a prefab floor is enough to fray anyone's nerves. So began a game of catch and tag, until eventually I would grab her and fling her onto the bed; then she would settle down again. This normally happened after my sense of humour had totally deserted me, especially as it became a nightly event.

As she grew up, Bok became destructive, preferring to eat washing rather than grass. She was eventually sent to a farm near the camp, and we hear she now sleeps happily in the dog house with the farm dog.

* * *

While much of our work away can be quite routine, there are some contracts that offer a dash of excitement, as was seen from my Mogadishu story, and as you will see from this one.

It's a typical day in Tanzania – sweltering heat, sounds of birds in the trees, humming of insects – and I'm relaxing in the clinic on a gold mine. Suddenly I'm rudely interrupted by a piercing alarm. I peer out of the window and notice that all hell has broken loose – the people on site are racing around frantically. I wonder if there's a major catastrophe on it's way. Intrigued, I watch more closely to see where they're actually running to – it's the smelt house! No-one is calling me on the radio and this intrigues me even more. It's then that I notice men in military-type uniforms emerging from everywhere. I'm certain this must be a coup and no-one has informed the medic – how inconsiderate!

I watch as people jump into vehicles amidst much yelling, whistling, screeching of tyres and that male bonding ritual of revving the hell out of the engines. I am torn away from my safe vantage point by a vehicle pulling up just outside the clinic, hooting for me! Rushing outside I notice someone in my land cruiser, dressed for Armageddon, yelling at me to "Get in!!!". Since he's the one with the rifle, I don't argue.

I notice that my vehicle is part of a convoy making its way to the landing strip. Trying to ignore my companion's wreckless driving, I ask what is going on. "This is the gold run," he says matter-of-factly. "The what?" I ask. "You know, the gold run …" he says. "No, I don't know the gold run!" I retort, somewhat impatient at not getting a proper answer and feeling I deserved one since I was now clearly a part of all this. "Why am I going to the gold run?" I try again, and this is when the driver drops the little gem, "Because they won't shoot the medic."

Apparently once a week, on a designated day known only to the financial manager and the mine manager, the gold run happens. The tiniest plane lands on our landing strip, but not before all the uniformed and heavily armed soldiers are strategically placed alongside the runway, hiding in the bushes with guns trained on the plane and runway. Then someone climbs out of the plane – today's 'mule' happens to be very scrawny. He is carrying two haversacks, one in front of him and one on his back. He is here to collect the gold bars from our smelt house.

Walking towards us, he proceeds to climb into my vehicle! For an operation that is clearly dangerous and kept hush-hush until the last minute, I find this more than disconcerting. With a huge paramedic symbol on the door telling everyone exactly where he is, we scream off to the smelt house.

Everyone is tense; much shouting is going on by men with more guns and shiny epaulettes. We get to the smelt house and I notice no-one is around except the soldiers; everyone else has vanished! So this is not a coup, but it feels just as dangerous. I try thinking back: I'm sure I never read anything about this in the handover notes. Funny that the medic before me forgot this small detail! It's even more interesting that my employers failed to mention this exciting weekly escapade.

I sit in the vehicle with two soldiers waiting for Scrawny to come out of the smelt house with the gold. Still very tense, no-one speaks, no-one lights cigarettes, no-one makes jokes, no-one discusses the lotto. We just sit in silence, no aircon, doors open, sweating. Even the birds are quiet. The doors of the smelt house finally burst open and out he comes, walking very slowly under the weight of the bars. I'm later told he has four bars in his bags.

Then, as if some invisible operator is pressing a replay button, it all starts again – shouting, yelling, revving of engines, and we're off to the landing strip. This time when we get there, it's even more tense. Scrawny is surrounded by four armed men and accompanied to the airplane steps. If anyone watching had any doubt about where the gold was, they'd only have to look at the little procession hurrying to the plane; very obvious, it's the only one there.

Finally, he's back in the plane, doors close, and everyone stands with bated breath – this is a crucial moment. The engines start and I am in my vehicle driving away from the airstrip. To anyone watching: Please notice that the medic is going back to the clinic so don't fire at her!

* * *

One December many years ago I did a short contract to fill in for a medic in Guinea who had taken ill. It took two days of travelling to get to the designated place. The company that I did this contract for always gets the medic a visa for neighbouring Liberia as well. On the fourth day of my shift the president of that country was shot. The next day the entire camp was packed up faster than you could say voyager miles, and we travelled by road to Liberia!! The president was from the very region we were in and it was feared that ethnic cleansing would follow.

* * *

On the high seas

Sometimes the site you are sent to is offshore on an oil rig or a ship. The shifts can vary from 28 days on shift and 28 off, or 6 weeks on and 6 weeks off, or even longer – 3 months on and one month off.

Offshore the medic never shares a cabin, which is great. However, you usually have other challenges because some ships are very small – the cabins are not spacious and have no facilities like TV, DVD, radio, Internet access or even a desk to work on.

To work offshore you need to go on the Helicopter Underwater Escape Training Course, which is a five-day course at the Institute of Maritime Studies in Cape Town. The course includes basic fire-fighting, updated CPR, how to deploy a life raft, procedures used at sea, deploying flares, the fire drill, and the man-overboard drill.

The course also included, as its name suggests, a series of thrilling underwater experiences – I can't believe I actually paid money to people who, after teaching the theory, proceeded to dump me in a simulated helicopter frame and, while wearing a seatbelt, turned me upside down in the water. Not just once, but three times!

If I close my eyes and think about it, I can torture myself all over again. Join me, all you brave hearts out there, sitting in your comfy chairs.

I'm dripping wet, waiting for the piece de resistance, which is escaping from the underwater capsule.

I've spent the past week learning how to sit in rescue launch crafts, how to set flares in case of emergency, and how to form a tight circle in the water with people in trouble, and wait for the rescue craft to pick us up. And now I'm about to learn how to escape from a helicopter under the water. Just written as words, it sounds as easy as saying "make a cup of tea".

But picture the North Sea, a heaving mass of freezing water. You're wearing a full-body insulated suit because the water is about four degrees, and hypothermia sets in very quickly. You're in the helicopter on your way to the rig when there's a problem and you feel the helicopter going down; now it's touching the water ... now it's under the water ... you have a safety belt on, and once you're under the water you have to count to ten, unstrap yourself and exit out of the nearest window ... now, wasn't that simple?

So now, while you're still astounded by my courage, let me tell you that no, this hasn't happened to me in the North Sea – yet. The training course was undertaken in slightly less dangerous waters in Cape Town but the procedure was the same. It was done in an indoor swimming pool with a suspended helicopter simulator capsule, which I had to climb into. Once in, you strap the safety belt on; one arm must be on the edge of the window pane and the other on the belt. You have to wait until the capsule is lowered under water, and when the water has engulfed you, count to ten and exit. We did this three times, with the capsule being turned at more of an angle each time until the capsule is upside-down.

I had a near-drowning experience as a child, so I found this quite tough. However, there were two divers in the water with us, in case people had panic attacks. Also, I was the only woman doing this course; but then, I've often been the only woman in a group of men doing a course. Some of them were divers and a lot fitter than I was. But I felt a lot better when the guy in front of me turned around and confided: "Guess what? I can't swim."

Once you're in a panic situation and have got as far as exiting through a window, the rush of water and consequent disorientation are nerve-wracking to say the least.

It's particularly life-threatening in the North Sea, which gets very rough because it's quite shallow – well, relatively speaking. It's nothing for 15-metre waves to lash the oil rigs, so one has to appreciate the skill of the pilots transporting people – both staff and patients. The helicopters can accommodate up to nine people in one flight, so it could be a total catastrophe if an accident should occur. That's why this training is essential.

Another requirement for working offshore is passing a strict medical examination to ensure that you're fit to work in offshore conditions.

* * *

It's a completely different way of life out there. Everyone is there to make money; companies spend an astronomical amount of money on safety, getting the work done and keeping its personnel safe. You are surrounded by water and usually don't see another living soul other than the people you work with. It's an incomparable way to really get to know people from other countries; here you don't just work with them, you go to the gym with them, eat with them, share cabins with them – you really get a feel for their culture and little idiosyncrasies.

I've worked for almost 15 years offshore now and have loved every minute of it. It is still a newish area for women, so it's still a novelty to see women on the platforms. I have always referred to the men whom I look after as 'my boys,' and being a woman, they usually come and chat to me. The younger ones see you as a bit of a mother figure; I can honestly say I've never felt threatened or unsafe out there.

Management is usually made up of very experienced men who have been in the field (or should I say water?) for many years. You might ask: "What does a medic do out there?" Apart from the obvious running of a clinic for any medical problems, we do many other things. For example – water sampling; hygiene inspections of the cabins, galleys and living quarters; and there are first aid and fire teams to train and update in the latest CPR techniques.

It is the medics' duty to train and educate all personnel on board about relevant issues such as malaria, healthy eating, and chest pain. There are meetings to attend every morning, and rescue plans to co-ordinate. And then, of course, it's always nice to get together with your colleagues who are also out at sea, and whinge about your day!

Out on the rigs there is a little more to do than in camps on dry land, many more meetings to attend, and constant testing of water. The medic is responsible for helping out with the flights that come in and booking the guys on the helicopter flight leaving the rig for shore.

Anyone who wants to use the gym on board must have an examination by the medic to pass as fit.

All personnel report to the medic so that we get a baseline medical history on them. I monitor patients who are on chronic medication and work out a programme for anyone who wants to lose weight.

* * *

Things can get hair-raising out on the high seas. One of my postings was on a survey vessel[26] en route from Mauritius to Dubai. This entails going through the most dangerous waters in the world because it is where pirates operate. Pirates hijack ships and keep the crew hostage while waiting for their ransom to be paid.

The Mogadishu Straits off Somalia are the worst. Every half an hour the captain on the bridge received a faxed status report of activities in and around the waters we were traversing. The maps laid out in the bridge had all the pirate activity marked with dates, including recommended routes to avoid areas of high activity.

On our ship measures were taken to minimize the chances of pirates boarding us. All crew had to do an hour or two of duty watch. Certain radars were switched off, radio use was kept to a minimum, barbed wire was strung up all around the ship, outside ladders were removed to well inside the ship; all doors from the outside were locked from the inside; only one door was allowed to be open. CCTV cameras were positioned at strategic points on the ship. We even made mannequins from cardboard stuffed into old boiler suits to make them look like real people, which we placed around the ship so that it looked like crew members on watch. We had endless drills on what to do in case of a pirate attack. In the event of an attack, an alarm is sounded, everyone

---

26 A vessel that searches the ocean bed for deposits of oil and or gas. It does this by shooting pockets of air over a large surface while the scientist on board read the data.

musters[27] and all crew members are checked to see that they have their life vest on. The medical team is assembled with equipment. Procedures are reiterated – stay low on deck, cover your head with both hands making sure your hands are visible, do not attempt to take pictures, do not make sudden movements, follow instructions at all times, do not confront anyone, do not stare at the pirates in a confrontational way. The captain would be increasing speed away from the oncoming attack, flares would be lit and deployed, fire pumps[28] normally used to extinguish fires on deck and kept at the ready for helicopter take-offs and landings would be activated and used to deflect any pirates attempting to board. The search lights would be switched on and directed at the pirates in an effort to blind them and stall for more escape time.

Community spirit

No matter where in the world you are, it's amazing how people pitch together to solve a problem when needed, helping in whatever way they can.

An incident I'll always fondly remember took place during my stint at a very small gold mine in Tanzania, hundreds of kilometres from anywhere and 20 kilometres from the Serengeti. The landing strip was rudimentary with no lights. The usual traffic on this strip was rush hour Africa-style – guinea fowl meandering along ahead of the occasional tortoise or small buck.

---

27   Meet at predetermined location
28   There is a maritime law against using any kind of fire weapon, such as guns, when defending a ship. The only weapon allowed is water sprayed at high speed.

As Murphy's Law would have it, nothing happened the entire four weeks that I was on site, but the day before I was due to fly out, it came down in a deluge.

There I was, sitting in my clinic, minding my own business as paramedics do, when I heard a voice on the radio yelling for the medic. No need to turn the volume up – I knew just by the tone of voice that this was an urgent call.

The manager's six-year-old son had been jumping on a trampoline and missed the side, partially amputating the little finger on his right hand.

The packaging of an amputated limb is vitally important. As mentioned before, you have only four hours from the time the limb is separated from the body to the time it is reattached – and that's the maximum time allowed[29]. When you have very poor communications, telephones that go down in the afternoon (a strange phenomenon I've only ever encountered in Tanzania) coupled with limited medical equipment, a very pale-looking child and an hysterical mother, the call becomes challenging to say the least.

News about our patient spread quickly and the flying doctors in Nairobi's world-renowned air mercy service were called. I was very worried about flying a patient to Nairobi for treatment as I had never been there and would rather he be flown to South Africa – but the sun would be going down soon and we couldn't affort to waste any time – every minute counted. The word was out: "Everyone with a vehicle, drive down to the landing strip immediately!"

There was much excitement as some people got only half the story and saw a large number of cars in mass exodus to the landing strip.

---

29   An amputated limb should be washed off to remove as much gross debris as possible, the wet end enclosed with a wet bandage, placed in a plastic container – a plastic bag is more than adequate – then placed in a container with ice.

And I'm sure many of the locals must have been wondering whether there was some major catastrophe afoot that they had not heard about, like an approaching meteorite.

The patient was a little star, a very pale star, but a wonderful patient nonetheless, being very brave for his mother and sister. Much of the time, all a person needs is someone else's touch, that magical touch that makes everything better.

In all the chaos, excitement and scurrying around I took a few moments to catch my breath and send out yet another silent prayer. I was on an embankment that overlooked the landing strip and in all my running around and treating the patient I hadn't seen how the people had rallied together for the little boy. I gazed down onto the landing strip and there were cars on either side, lined up next to each other, ready to put their lights on for the plane. I looked closely and got gooseflesh – in amongst the expats from our camp were locals who worked on the mine, standing between the vehicles holding LCD lights that could be plugged in. I caught a glimpse of the camp manager – he was handing out torches. I saw the security guard holding a hand-held gas lamp; the cleaner who burned the kitchen rubbish was holding a gas lamp and talking to the little patient sitting on his mother's lap. The selflessness was overwhelming. I am reminded that, no matter what, people will always stand together when something is important enough. The human spirit triumphs in so many ways. It's a beautiful thing to see.

The plane arrived as the sun was going down, and the pilot was very impressed and grateful for the well-lit landing strip.

On my next trip back, I was greeted by my little patient running up to hug me, yelling "Look at my finger!" It was fully functional, had beautiful colour and a thin red line at the base where it had been reattached.

Being away from home

Personnel who work away and offshore give up a tremendous number of things that are taken for granted by our families and friends back home. We work hard, long hours in severe conditions; and we sleep in bunks and uncomfortable beds. Sometimes we sleep in hotels, which might sound glamorous, but there is no getting up in the middle of the night for a midnight snack or even to switch on the light and read. You simply don't do it because you would be disturbing the person sharing your cabin. And even if you have your own room or unit, it's not home. There is no couch to nod off on while watching TV; no familiar smells of home; no warm body to snuggle up to at night; no loving canine with soft ears sleeping at your feet; no familiar bed linen such as your favourite pillow or duvet. You just can't bring much with you because often luggage is severely restricted, particularly if your transfer to site is by small fixed-wing aircraft or helicopter. Meals are shared with a bunch of people who most often don't even speak your language. Eating is never a slow, enjoyable affair anyway; mealtimes are always rushed as production never stops for one minute.

The companies that own the huge oil rigs really go out of their way to make it as comfortable as they can, but it's still not home. You get to miss out on so many things with your family – your childrens' first day at school; the loss of the first tooth; their learning to ride a bicycle; the excitement of the dog giving birth to puppies; and new neighbours moving in next door.

I have seen a lot of marriages and relationships fall apart. It's very tough for two people to live apart and yet stay close. If your relationship isn't secure, it is easy to become overly worried, even paranoid, about what your partner back home is up to; and the partner at home often grows tired of spending nights alone, shouldering the day-to-day responsibility of running the family home alone, and not having their partner around to share in all the special occasions and help with decisions. Regular communication may or may not be easy – depending on where you are based. Some couples just can't do it and very often the person at home is the one who throws in the towel and decides to move on. I can tell you this from first-hand, extremely painful experience. I can honestly say that was the darkest hour of my life. I was working on an oil rig; I had travelled there on my birthday and just before I came home for Christmas, my partner of eight years decided that she'd had enough. It was all over – just like that.

Every one of us who works away is there for the money and nothing else. The sacrifice I've made has enabled me to send my children to a really good school and never want for anything. It has afforded me a lifestyle I would never have had as a paramedic working only in South Africa. Although I long to be back home full time where I can enjoy the emotional continuity and warmth of a close, loving relationship, spend more time with the people that matter to me and be a part of all the special occasions and events that pass me by, this is what I have to do for now. I do not regret my choice. But I do look forward to coming home and diving back into the work I love so much, and shaping the minds of new paramedics through lecturing and sharing my knowledge with passion.

* * *

11

Epilogue

I have many more stories that keep me company, but I have told the most important ones – the ones that give you a glimpse of the best and sometimes the worst of being human.

And if you had to peek inside my mind you would see that all these stories are like a spider web; they cannot be separated from everyday life. Touch one thread and all the rest will quiver. There is always a smell, a gesture, a look, a tone that I connect with, or that reminds me of something I've done, read, seen or experienced. It's impossible to touch that web without it setting off a gentle tremor.

It's my sincere hope that you enjoyed reading these tales as much I have enjoyed relating them. All humans will die of hypoxia one day – not enough oxygen to the brain – that is a given, it's unavoidable. So it's important that what we have to say in the time we are alive has real meaning. For in the words I write, I will continue to live.

I've let you share my innermost perceptions, feel my sadness, laugh with me. And I've given you insight into a place you've probably never before thought of. It's probably a bit like meeting someone who lives in a lighthouse. I've always wondered who does that kind of work, what makes them want to be so isolated, what do they do all day?

In my words the spirits of medics before me and after me live on. The next time you see a paramedic at a scene, I hope you will view them in a different light. You now know they made that career choice not for money but for the love of service; know they work while you sleep; know they get soaked working in the rain; and tired after very long shifts; and know they too get mad at parents who don't strap in their kids. They are just like you, but trained to work in extreme conditions and deal with humans facing their rawest moments and emotions, daily.

And remember the Saturday Night Show, brought to you by the citizens of Joburg ...

* * *

About the author

Bruna Dessena is an Advanced Life Support (ALS) Paramedic who currently does shift work abroad managing remote-site clinics. While her work has taken her all over the world and exposed her to many interesting assignments and opportunities, the bulk of her career has seen her working in and around Johannesburg, known for it's high crime and busy hospital casualties.

Bruna is a lecturer/instructor in various aspects of emergency medicine and teaches medical and company staff both on site where she works, and in various training colleges back home in Cape Town, where she now resides with her partner. She maintains her 'on-the-road' emergency skills by volunteering her services to a community-based and sponsored medical emergency service in Hout Bay, and by doing stand-in shifts for various emergency services companies in and around Cape Town and Johannesburg.

Bruna was a volunteer counsellor for both Childline and the Teddy Bear Clinic. At the latter she was also a trainer and Senior Facilitator preparing children and parents for court. She currently presents lectures on child abuse to paramedics and doctors, as well as med-school, nursing and social work students at various universities, colleges and hospitals in the Western Cape and Johannesburg. Bruna also conducts talks for teachers and parents at schools in and around the Western Cape.

Bruna has two children, Themba and Khangiswe. In 2016, she obtained her Masters in Emergency Medicine focusing on child abuse disclosure during medical treatment, and has published a second book, *Every Parent's Nightmare: The Adults' Guide to Dealing with Child Abuse.*

Other titles by the author

Every Parent's Nightmare
ISBN 978-0-620-46292-1

Every Parent's Nightmare is a practical guide for anyone dealing with suspected or confirmed child abuse.

It will help you:

- understand more about paedophiles and the grooming process
- know which children are more at risk of being abused
- identify the signs of abuse
- understand more about online bullying and cybergrooming
- address the problem with the child if you suspect abuse
- support the child when you find out or if the child discloses
- understand the legal process involved and the important steps to take when abuse has been disclosed
- know what goes into preparing children for court
- learn how to keep your child safe.

It includes the Sexual Offences Act and the Children's Act so that adults and caregivers know what the child's rights are and what one can expect from the legal system in South Africa. It also includes handy resources and contact numbers for counselling and support.

Also available at:
www.publisher.co.za
www.every-parents-nightmare.com

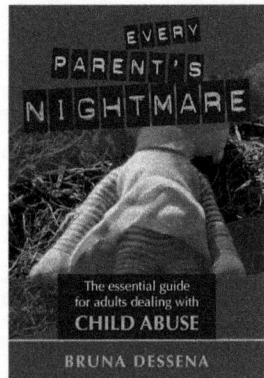

www.ingramcontent.com/pod-product-compliance
Lightning Source LLC
LaVergne TN
LVHW041221080426
835508LV00011B/1030